ACTIVITY BOOK
FOR INMATES

CONTENT

HOW TO PLAY

A word search puzzle is a word game that consists of the letters of words placed in a grid, which usually has a rectangular or square shape.
The objective of this puzzle is to find and mark all the words hidden inside the box.
The words may be placed horizontally, vertically, or diagonally.
Often a list of the hidden words is provided, but more challenging puzzles may not provide a list.
Many word search puzzles have a theme to which all the hidden words are related such as food, animals, or colors.

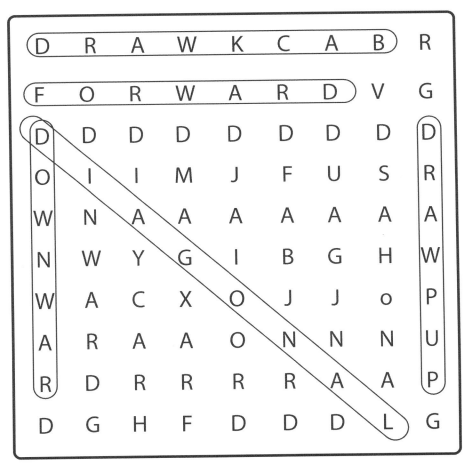

Words to find

BACKWARD	DIAGONAL	UPWARD
FORWARD	DOWNWARD	

Puzzle # 1 WILD

DEVILMENT
AEGILOPS
BUTTERCUP
WANTON
GUANACO
CRITTER
GENTLE
MERRY
CHASE
DEBAUCH
OREGANO
LIVE
ORIGINAL
RAGGED
EERY
SCENE
RAVER
DOMESTICATE
TRAMMEL
MADNESS

```
T S L M K P O L I G E A P G C
M A D E S O R M I R P C O J G
C T E D O M E S T I C A T E P
E R V G T P G H D U R F N T R
O R I G I N A L T R I T A T I
S G L T Z L N R E N L U W I S
W C M R T M O M D Z I B E R M
V A E G B E Y P R R E C R C A
N E N N L R R S S E N D A M R
B U T T E R C U P V R A V Y K
T D N E O Y H T R A M M E L H
I E O C A N A U G R U E S N O
G V R C H A S G U A N A C B R
E F L I V D E B A U C H N E I
S C E N V D E V I L M E N Z Y
```

Puzzle # 2 TRUCK

BATCH
DOLLY
TRUCKER
TRAILER
ROLLBACK
HEADLIGHT
STEAMROLLER
FORESTAY
GHARRY
FLOAT
SHIP
TAILBOARD
MOGUL
HIJACK
THRIVING
PICKUP
FREIGHTAGE
NARRATION
GEARSHIFT
BARELY

```
N S R R H T R U C K E G I A G
O A W T K E N A R R A T I O N
A Y R A V T E E G E P B A T I
S R L I R H R E L I A R T D V
D H R L B M A U C T B E O E I
U D I B O U Y K C A B L L O R
M U T O G D U H H K L L O A H
P R R A I P T E C P E O Y R T
S B A R E L Y A T S E R O F R
T A I D R A J D I S R M V L U
E T L E M I F L O A T A R O N
R C E O H A P I H S E E R A D
H W G D E M O G U L O T A G L
A U G E A R S H I F T S H T E
A F R E I G H T A G E W G D D
```

Puzzle # 3 JEWELRY

NECKWEAR
DISPLAY
ARTISAN
AMULET
BEAU
SILVER
BAUBLE
METAL
MISANTHROPE
SPLENDID
PASTE
PEBBLE
BROOCH
RHODIUM
TASSEL
FANCY
FILIGREE
JEWELER
HEIRLOOM
SOLITAIRE

```
C I D N E L P S M E T A R B E
F J I T J O P P O N S R A N M
N E D L A E B L O O E U E E R
E W N I B M A K L L B C P C E
S E E B S P U O R L K T O K E
O L L G H P B L I W T B R W R
L E P U S I L V E R Y H H E G
I R S A M I E A H T O C T A I
T A O A S A R D Y D O A N G L
A A S P C T A U I O S S A A I
I A S A I S X U R S O K S B F
R U A S I E M B E C R E I P F
E L A T E M E Q D O E T M I S
A N R E U L A V D I S P L A O
C A S C B S I L V E G U I E C
```

Puzzle # 4 BALLOON

ASCENSIONAL
FANTASTIC
ELASTICITY
BALLOONING
INTENDED
ASCENT
DOPE
BAREFOOT
DRIFT
WAFT
IMMOVABLE
KEEL
DEFLATE
ENVELOPE
INFLATABLE
LIFT
TURGID
NACELLE
ASCENSION
MONTGOLFIER

```
F A A A P E R S U A S I V E R
A S E E E L B A T A L F N I R
B C D R R P G L U F T N E V E
T E I O T I O D D R I F N F I
I N G N O A W L O L N A F I F
C D R A O A B Y E P T E A M L
I I U U F S A T R V E L N M O
T N T T E C L I F W N L T O G
S G F S R E L C O S D E A V T
A I I L A N O I S N E C S A N
L X R A B T O T Y I D A T B O
E P D O P N N S R F I N I L M
A S C E N B I A E T A L F E D
T U R G I Q N L F E F W C E C
A S C E U R G E S R C E E K I
```

Puzzle # 5 — SCHOOL LUNCH IDEAS

OBSTINACY
FOGGY
MODERNITY
GESTATE
PRIMARY
AUDITORY
TRACK
ICONOCLAST
CONTENTION
ICKY
AIKIDO
BRAIN
HOME
GROUND
MISOCAINEA
NONSENSICAL
JUNIOR
INNOVATION
STUDENT
HAIL

```
L C H S T U D E N T S G C E R
N A O F O G G Y O K R H A Y Y
I P M N L N I C C O O S E X S
N I E E T P S A U M E T N T D
N R M O D E R N I T Y I I I I
O E C O N T N I A C A N A N G
V C R S D I L T M P K V C R E
A E Y R A C S S I A L Y O E S
T P T R A E N B R O R U S D T
I T B R G B D O I O N Y I O I
O I T O N N I K T D D I M M O
N O N S E N S I C A L I A H N
E N N A U U D I K I A I K A T
K A E J B U G G O F B R A I J
S U T S A L C O N O C I N V A
```

Puzzle # 6 — TOMATO

GREEN
ASPIC
PLANT
MARENGO
TORPEDO
MYOPIC
APPLE
SOLANACEOUS
VINE
NIGHTSHADE
BRUISE
PHYSALIS
SLIP
TOMATILLO
ENCOURAGE
BASIL
SPHINX
HEATED
PASTA
RETARDATION

```
T I L W H R A A S P I K T R S
O N T E E N C O U R A G E L Y
M O E O N D G N O B R U I S F
V R L T L N G M E S I U R B P
G A P O E L A E C A P E B R N
I C L R R C I E A H E A T E D
T A A P P L E T N D S P O T M
T M N E E R G I A I A P R A Y
E A T D T O V H L M V L P R O
H R H O N I S A O Y O R E D P
G E Y A G T S P S O P T D A I
A N R A H Y H A H P H A Y T Y
P G T G H Y N S B I I G L I D
S L I P P A S T E C N C I O P
T N A R G P L A N F P X Y N S
```

Puzzle # 7   TRAIN

CRUPPER
QUADRATE
HEADWAY
MEET
TRAMMEL
FUSE
TRACTION
HANDLER
TRAINLOAD
LUNGE
PRACTISE
CARSICK
LOOKOUT
ORIGINATE
DERAILMENT
RIDER
JUDO
CAVALCADE
FINISH
UTILITY

```
D L C R U P P E G S H D O S O
U S E H E A D W A G S R M I A
T V L E E T N E M L I A R E D
I B O A R R F H C G N O C O E
L O O K O U T A I R I B N C T
I L K E S T R N L F F Q R H R
T U O L M S A D U A L U E S A
Y N U E I T C L N R P A S S I
E G L C E N T E G P D D I E N
Q U K R E D I R E W W R T N L
U K D J U D O R A G E A C R O
A E U R S O N Y T M E T A E A
Y D T S E F I N A M M E R V D
K I I C A V A L C A D E P O N
T R A C T I O M N A T M L G L
```

Puzzle # 8   FOUNDATION

JUDAISM
CULVERT
RUDIMENTARY
UPSET
GROUNDING
BASIC
COFFERDAM
LIBRARY
ROCK
HENRY
CEREMONY
FUNDING
CORSELET
COMMONER
BASEBOARD
LECTURESHIP
AIRY
PATTEN
ROOT
BERM

```
U L R M G L I B R A R I C O N
T A R E N O M M O C L U U N N
U T I L I T Y Y I I B A L E D
I N B K D I C N L E H B V T R
L E A O N Q C O R S E L E T A
E M S R U C S M F R N Y R A O
C A I G F P E E V F R R B P B
T D J C N C S R D S E A B J E
U N R U D I M E N T A R Y S S
R U O L D S D C T I N B D I A
E F C V H A L N R R T I I A B
S E K E I B I A U O J L L D M
H E N R Y J U S T O O U O U I
I T Y T Y I B F M T R X S J E
P A T T E W M U P S E G S A M
```

Puzzle # 9   ARMY TRAINING

PROVO
VARLET
EDUCATED
DRUMHEAD
ESOTERIC
REPUBLICAN
REARGUARD
MEDIC
INTERNSHIP
BASIC
REGIMEN
DISCIPLINED
CONSULTANT
BREEDING
FARTLEK
ARTILLERY
PULLOUT
SIMULATION
THERAPY
SQUAD

```
B W G S I M U L A T I O N R A
D P A N Z E R N P U L L O U T
D A C N I B A S I C S Q U A F
O R U O G D L E H A L A B E R
D T U Q N L E Y S D R A E E R
R I R Y S S E E N O S T G F N
D L S A S L U T R I H I E A L
R L E C R H H L E B M O C R L
A E E A I E S O T E R I C T E
U R V D R P V C N A L E U L B
G Y E A U O L I I B N W W E B
R M P P R E G I U D B T M K M
A Y C P U L E P N I E L M U U
E D U C A T E D A E H M U R D
R E G V O R P T M R D E E Z R
```

Puzzle # 10   GRADUATE

HOFFMAN
TRIBE
EDUCATE
MARKETABLE
JUBILANT
INTERN
ERSTWHILE
INTERNSHIP
HIGHTAIL
DIPLOMA
CONTINUUM
MEDICINE
CLERK
TENURE
EXPECT
GRADUATED
CALIBRATION
SEDUCE
COURSE
CONVOCATION

```
C O N V O C A T I O N C J S E
U N O I T A R B I L A C U L G
N R P E C N E C U D E S B A A
A N H I M O A X E I E A K F L
L A T I H B R L P B T A P E L
I M C R G S I Z I E A E M H O
B F U R G H N R K B C U R C C
U F D E W R T R T M U T E O T
J O E T G T A A E N D J L U C
K H S N P M I D I T E N U R E
P R O I O R I T U L N M F S P
E S E L E C N E R A N I M E S
H G P L I O H I G H T A I H O
C I C N C Z T A C U D E E D R
D H E H O F F M A H M E D E P
```

Puzzle # 11 SHARK

MAKO
DEMOISELLE
SELACHIAN
CHAGRIN
DUSKY
TOPE
HAMMER
SAILFISH
LANDLORD
THRESHER
ISURUS
THRASHER
MONSTER
RHINCODON
DORSAL
CURIOSITY
PANGA
BONNETHEAD
SHARK
FISH

```
B A B D R O L D N A L R D N O
D U S K E G U M M Y R H P I E
E T H R M M A K O A S R O D O
M Z K A M I O P A N G A T R R
O L C H A G R I N R S G H H H
B T A S H D D U S K Y T R C I
E W H U O D F A C E A S E U N
N N E R N A I H C A L E S R C
C P S U A L S A I X P L H I O
H A R S F S C M K O B I E O D
L S H I R K H M T T N H R S O
E N S B O N N E T H E A D I N
Y H S I F T A C R R B W L T U
S E L A C H I A R P I K T Y M
N H N D E M O I S E L L S D C
```

Puzzle # 12 ORIGINAL

APHORISM
GENUINE
CLOVE
SPRINGY
PRIMER
UNWORN
ADOPTED
DEFLECT
CLASSICALLY
SCARCE
ETYMON
CLONE
CONSEQUENT
FUNDAMENTAL
TAKEOFF
MINT
RESTORER
STEAL
TRIPLE
IMAGINATIVE

```
P R I M E E L A M I R P S V L
S S S N S C A R C F R T S F N
Y C P O C H P R N I E E C U I
N N R M E L H R M A R L L N M
S I I Y E S O E L O O E A D A
I U N T T W R V D N T T V A G
R N G E N U I N E L S Y E M I
O E Y U E I S S T T E M M E N
H G T A U R M C P C R O I N A
P C P T Q P T A O V E I R T T
A H S T E A P R D R I L P A I
A C L A S S I C A L L Y F L V
U R O W N U D E S C E N T E E
T A K E O F F S P R I N G S D
J V O L C U N P L O U G H E D
```

Puzzle # 13   RELATIONSHIPS

NOMOGRAM
TAXONOMIST
ETHNOLOGY
RELATE
MATCHMAKER
ALLUSION
PROXEMICS
CASE
MATHEMATICS
ANTISOCIAL
STRUMPET
FAST
PERSON
POLYGAMOUS
TAXONOMY
HOMOGENY
BEDROOM
PARSE
HIPSTER
NICHE

```
G R A M M A R G M A S N M L C
O H H T A L E R O U F I L N N
L O Y I P L C W O F C D O O Y
A M N T P B I M R S M R S M S
R F E A F S A C D R P R Y A C
U A G X D G T A E A E F I L I
T S O O Y Y T E B P S L A M T
C T M L N P G A R C A I A S A
U E O H E E E O X L C R H T M
R P H U S H X R L O G R S G E
T M U H T E C U S O N Y A E H
S U Y C M T S I M O N O X A T
T R C I S I T O N U T H M T A
R T C N O N N M A T C V T Y M
L S H N A M A T C H M A K E R
```

Puzzle # 14   BABY SHOWER

BARREN
LOST
BREASTFEED
OBSTETRICS
WAGON
ODDBALL
HENCE
CHICKEN
PATRICIDE
ATTENTION
STORK
MAMMAL
SLUICE
STERILIZE
THROW
UNBORN
SNUG
HOLLY
OWLET
SPARKLER

```
L L L A B D D O D D B A L K D
A O O B S T E T R I C N A E S
R T S N E T S I R H C C R P S
U O T P C N E H E B E R A T H
D D O E U U S R L D A N O D O
I D R O N L L E I B G R C D L
P L K F U T U C S L F U R E L
E E T I H Y I C C H I C K E N
E R C R L R C O A T S Z D F N
W Z O L T S E I N O W L E T S
A E O A C H I C K E F W S S Y
G H P M N U N B O R N O G A W
O B T M S P A R K L E R U E C
B R E A S T F E E Z C H N R E
W S B M P S C I R T E T S B O
```

Puzzle # 15   PERSONAL FINANCE

DUFFEL
TERTIARY
RESOURCE
HIDE
STAKE
PRINCIPLED
IMPERSONAL
INVISIBLE
INTEREST
COMMENTARY
HIRE
GOOD
RELIGION
LUST
DEVISE
DISCOUNT
MONIKER
BANKROLL
MEDIUM
SUITE

```
D H H W H T E R T I A R F E F
N O I G I L E R C D J E I D A
S K D D R V U C I S R N E M C
S T A K E E R S U S V L C O H
E F C N S U C L T I P O O D X
L R U Y O O L A S I M G D S B
E E E S U O K I C M E D I U M
C T E N R V B N E P E D V I V
A R T K C L I N T E R E S T E
F F N T E R T I A R Y S E E F
I A F F P A H K G S Y I R G F
B N F A R E K I N O M V E D U
B U T Y I K S E R N O E T U D
D A F F A I R E G A W D N B R
D O P R I N C I P L E H I T R
```

Puzzle # 16   SMARTPHONE

SCRAMBLE
SWISH
BEAT
COOKIE
PREDICTIVE
LICK
PERK
NUMERAL
SPRUCE
DINKY
INCENSED
SCREEN
LOCKED
SNAPPER
TONE
FORGIVABLE
BRAW
NADIR
SALVAGEABLE
CALLBACK

```
U Y T I R U C E S N I L W S S
E R F K S I N C E N S E F P W
E E C O C P A T O N A D I R I
R V N S R O R P E S W P E U S
I I K U A G O U E L S A P C H
N E N L M L I K C R G K R E P
C C I L B E V V I V T A E B R
E E D H L Y R A A D M L I C K
N R E P L K I A G B V F K A Q
S C R E E N O T L E L A O L E
E V I T C I D E R P A E O I E
D I R S S D E K C O L B C C R
S T U P I D K K C A B L L A C
B R A F W T E L E P H O N E S
P E R E S P R E D I C T I V Q
```

Puzzle # 17   TRAIL RUNNING

CURRICULUM
ARCHITRAVE
POSSE
BACKPACKER
SEEDY
WHIPCORD
DROOL
CONCOMITANT
EDDY
SKYWRITING
FUSE
OVERSEER
NAIL
OBLIQUE
BREAK
TACKLE
OPERATION
SPRAG
RUFFLE
GULCH

```
W H I G J N B N S R O H G U O
N A M D T N A T I M O C N O C
F A E E K I C I A V L L I G N
U E I D V H K S L C L U T L A
S E C D A O P O S S Z G I L R
E D O P E R A T I O N Q R K O
U D L P A M C N W P R A W C C
Q C D G U I K H H E E E Y A P
I O K Y D E E S I U E R K T I
L N I K A E R B P T S B S A H
B V I G M U L U C I R R U C W
O U I F F D R O O L E A C K A
A L U F R Z O O R D V E V L K
W S L S P R A E D P O S S E A
V E F O O T I N G R U F F L Z
```

Puzzle # 18   MOBILE

JAILBREAK
MOUSE
SIGNAL
TOLUENE
BOOM
ROAM
BURNER
SKID
DOCK
THAW
DISCO
UNBLOCK
FEELER
TRAILER
SYNC
INTERFACE
RAFT
LANDLINE
DOLLY
STREAM

```
B O O C S I D I K S Y N C C F
I O A F K A E R B L I A J M K
R M R C E S P D I U T G K T D
A T O L U E N E N C R E N H Y
F D A O N L L E T U J N O A L
M N M R B T D E E L A I E W L
X O U D L L N T R A I L E R O
S B U I O E T I F M L D C R D
Y T G S C C E O A A B N C T O
N H E C K L I E C E R A O R L
T O L U E N R A E T E L L A L
D F A E R T S N T H A L B I R
L B F T S K I G O A D K N L E
D S T R E A M I N G A L U E R
A C E T O N T S E D L O A X E
```

Puzzle # 19   AIRCRAFT

CANOPY
GYROPLANE
DEBARK
PLANE
WAKE
BIRD
FLEET
TURBOFAN
CLEARANCE
DISEMBARK
AUTOGIRO
DROP
OUTBOARD
ARMAMENT
KILL
HOLD
HIGHFLIER
SHED
BUFFET
CANNON

```
D N C N A R A E L C G O R U T
R B P L A N U L B D N H G H U
O U S D E H S I W I I Y N I R
G F H I G A T T U L R S I G B
Y F O S D N R A N O O D D H O
R E R E K Y F A P E O H L F F
O A I M R P F L N S M C O L A
P P G B A O A L E C R A H I H
L T O A B N U I E E E N M E E
A B T R E A R T R E T N K R C
N C U K D C S H B S S O R G A
F T A F I K O H O O C N Y O N
K W L E F L S T E W A R D K O
A I R P D E L S C I I R E A P
K E F B I R T U R A B E D W C
```

Puzzle # 20   EARTHQUAKE

SEISM
ROCK
PHENOMENON
LIFE
PALLET
DEVASTATE
OAKLAND
DISRUPTION
CHASM
INTENSITY
TREMOR
EPICENTRE
SPUR
APOCALYPSE
TREMBLER
DISTURBANCE
BEFALL
EARTHQUAKE
QUAKE
TSUNAMI

```
E C N A B R U T S I D C A A P
A F O T R E M B L E R N P N C
R O C G C H A S V B E O D O S
T S U N A M I A E W C I A I U
H E E K A H S F C A N K S T B
Q G R P P T A A L T L C P P D
U A T M A L S Y E A H O U U U
A R N T L T P N N I P R B R C
K O E C L S S D A L R U P S T
E H C E E I E P I O K T N I I
S C I K T C F F M R S R S D O
H N P Y A P H E N O M E N O N
A A E N T U R A P U I M I P I
K D E V V T Q V S S T O K S T
H E E P A L L E M M A X O H Q
```

HOW TO PLAY

The only available information are numbers telling you how many ship segments are in each row and column, and some given ship segments in various places in the grid.

The object is to discover where all ten ships are located in the grid.

The fleet consists of
1. battleship (4 squares)
2. cruisers (3 squares)
3. destroyers (2 squares)
4. submarines (1 squares)

A solid block signifies a middle part of a ship.

A curved shape signifies the start or the end of a ship.

The ships may be oriented horizontally and/or vertically in the grid, but not diagonally.

Ships can not occupy adjacent grid squares, even diagonally.

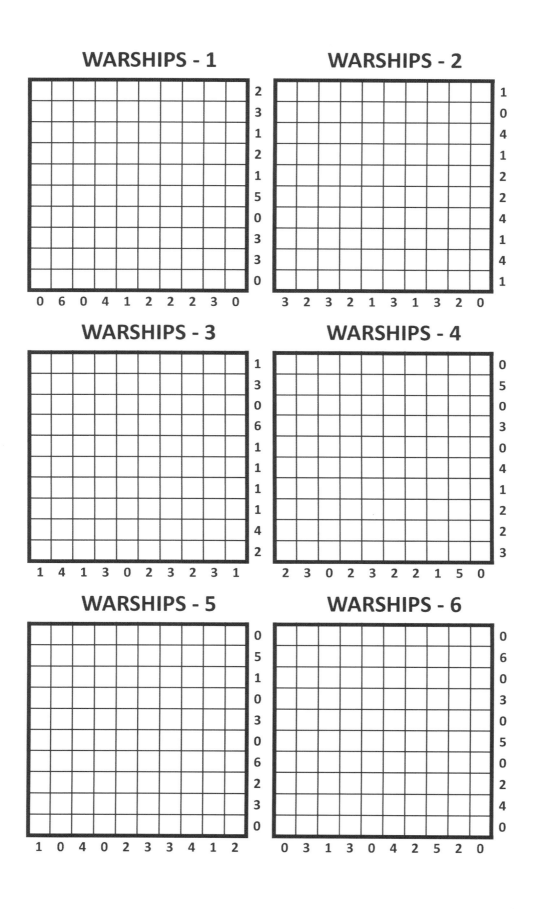

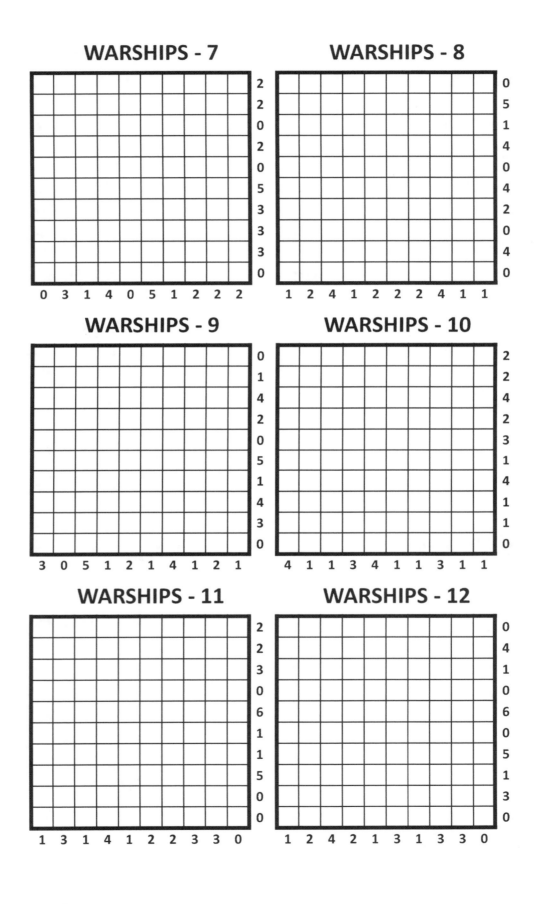

WARSHIPS - 7

Right side: 2 2 0 2 0 5 3 3 3 0
Bottom: 0 3 1 4 0 5 1 2 2 2

WARSHIPS - 8

Right side: 0 5 1 4 0 4 2 0 4 0
Bottom: 1 2 4 1 2 2 2 4 1 1

WARSHIPS - 9

Right side: 0 1 4 2 0 5 1 4 3 0
Bottom: 3 0 5 1 2 1 4 1 2 1

WARSHIPS - 10

Right side: 2 2 4 2 3 1 4 1 1 0
Bottom: 4 1 1 3 4 1 1 3 1 1

WARSHIPS - 11

Right side: 2 2 3 0 6 1 1 5 0 0
Bottom: 1 3 1 4 1 2 2 3 3 0

WARSHIPS - 12

Right side: 0 4 1 0 6 0 5 1 3 0
Bottom: 1 2 4 2 1 3 1 3 3 0

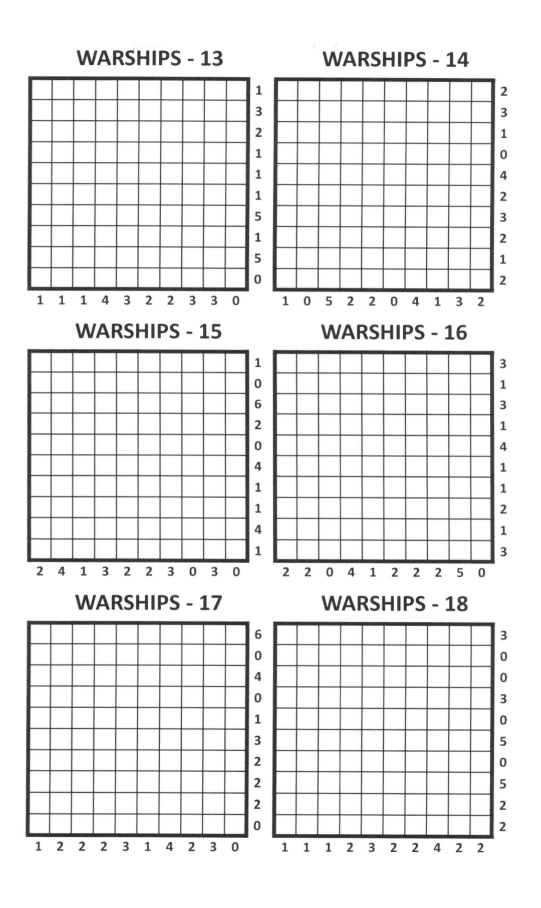

WARSHIPS - 13

Right: 1 3 2 1 1 1 5 1 5 0
Bottom: 1 1 1 4 3 2 2 3 3 0

WARSHIPS - 14

Right: 2 3 1 0 4 2 3 2 1 2
Bottom: 1 0 5 2 2 0 4 1 3 2

WARSHIPS - 15

Right: 1 0 6 2 0 4 1 1 4 1
Bottom: 2 4 1 3 2 2 3 0 3 0

WARSHIPS - 16

Right: 3 1 3 1 4 1 1 2 1 3
Bottom: 2 2 0 4 1 2 2 2 5 0

WARSHIPS - 17

Right: 6 0 4 0 1 3 2 2 2 0
Bottom: 1 2 2 2 3 1 4 2 3 0

WARSHIPS - 18

Right: 3 0 0 3 0 5 0 5 2 2
Bottom: 1 1 1 2 3 2 2 4 2 2

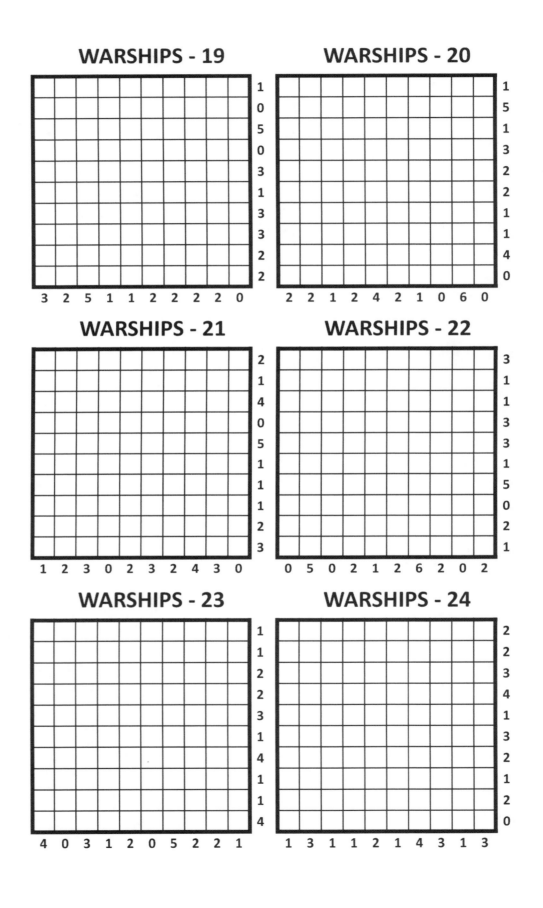

WARSHIPS - 19

Right: 1 0 5 0 3 1 3 3 2 2
Bottom: 3 2 5 1 1 2 2 2 2 0

WARSHIPS - 20

Right: 1 5 1 3 2 2 1 1 4 0
Bottom: 2 2 1 2 4 2 1 0 6 0

WARSHIPS - 21

Right: 2 1 4 0 5 1 1 1 2 3
Bottom: 1 2 3 0 2 3 2 4 3 0

WARSHIPS - 22

Right: 3 1 1 3 3 1 5 0 2 1
Bottom: 0 5 0 2 1 2 6 2 0 2

WARSHIPS - 23

Right: 1 1 2 2 3 1 4 1 1 4
Bottom: 4 0 3 1 2 0 5 2 2 1

WARSHIPS - 24

Right: 2 2 3 4 1 3 2 1 2 0
Bottom: 1 3 1 1 2 1 4 3 1 3

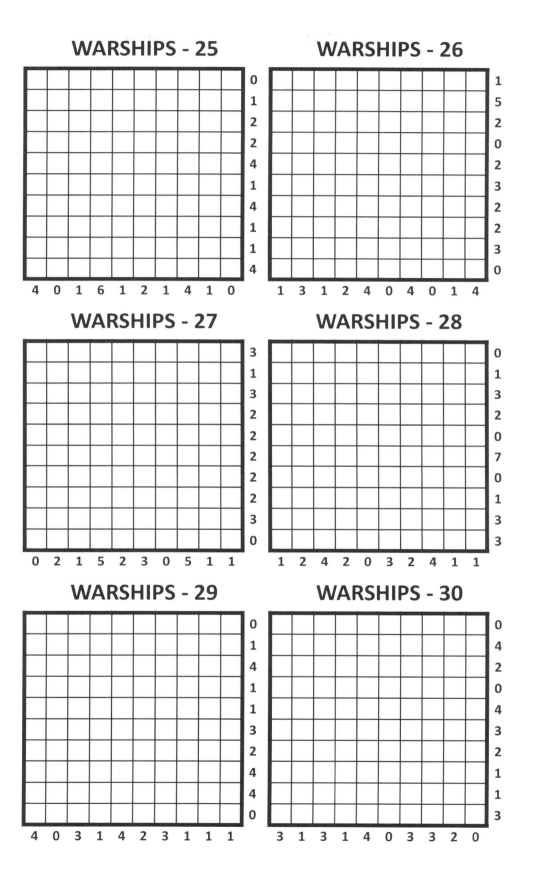

WARSHIPS - 25

Right: 0 1 2 2 4 1 4 1 1 4
Bottom: 4 0 1 6 1 2 1 4 1 0

WARSHIPS - 26

Right: 1 5 2 0 2 3 2 2 3 0
Bottom: 1 3 1 2 4 0 4 0 1 4

WARSHIPS - 27

Right: 3 1 3 2 2 2 2 2 3 0
Bottom: 0 2 1 5 2 3 0 5 1 1

WARSHIPS - 28

Right: 0 1 3 2 0 7 0 1 3 3
Bottom: 1 2 4 2 0 3 2 4 1 1

WARSHIPS - 29

Right: 0 1 4 1 1 3 2 4 4 0
Bottom: 4 0 3 1 4 2 3 1 1 1

WARSHIPS - 30

Right: 0 4 2 0 4 3 2 1 1 3
Bottom: 3 1 3 1 4 0 3 3 2 0

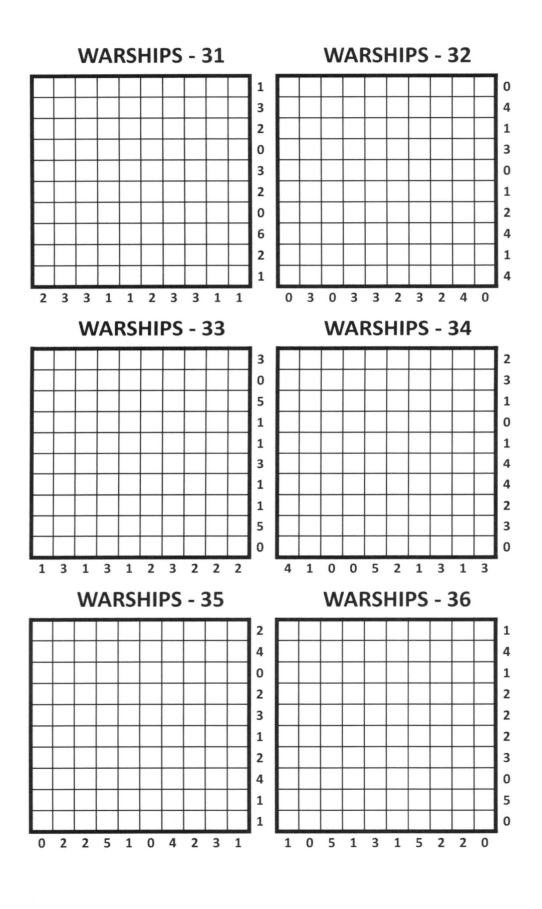

WARSHIPS - 37

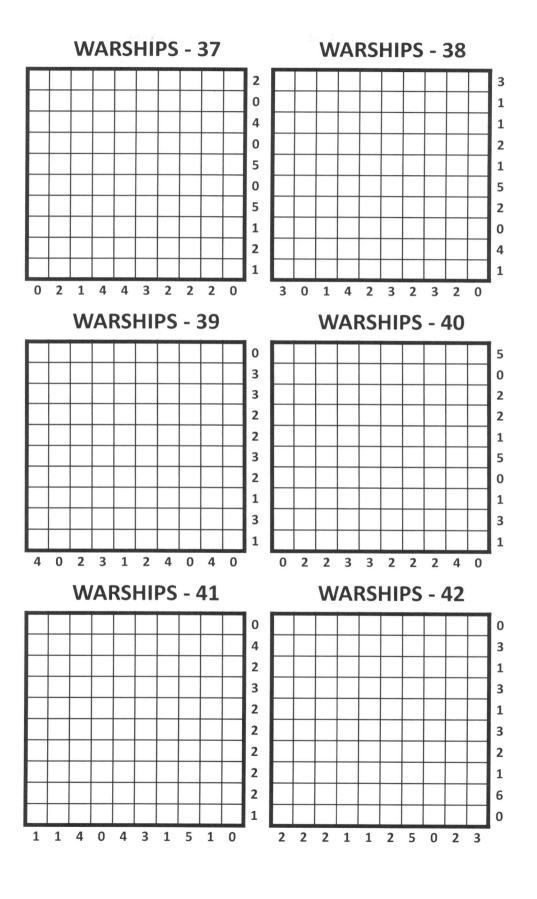

Right column: 2 0 4 0 5 0 5 1 2 1
Bottom row: 0 2 1 4 4 3 2 2 2 0

WARSHIPS - 38

Right column: 3 1 1 2 1 5 2 0 4 1
Bottom row: 3 0 1 4 2 3 2 3 2 0

WARSHIPS - 39

Right column: 0 3 3 2 2 3 2 1 3 1
Bottom row: 4 0 2 3 1 2 4 0 4 0

WARSHIPS - 40

Right column: 5 0 2 2 1 5 0 1 3 1
Bottom row: 0 2 2 3 3 2 2 2 4 0

WARSHIPS - 41

Right column: 0 4 2 3 2 2 2 2 2 1
Bottom row: 1 1 4 0 4 3 1 5 1 0

WARSHIPS - 42

Right column: 0 3 1 3 1 3 2 1 6 0
Bottom row: 2 2 2 1 1 2 5 0 2 3

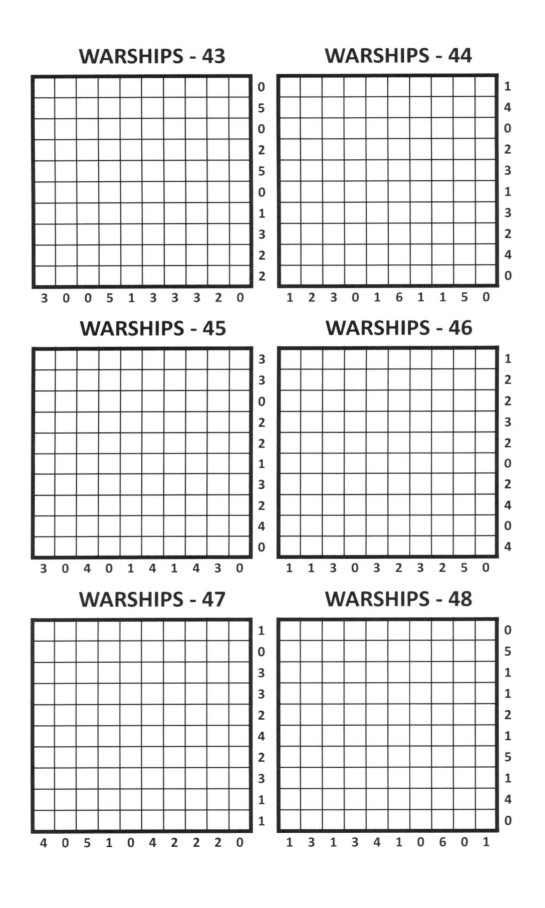

WARSHIPS - 43

Right side: 0 5 0 2 5 0 1 3 2 2
Bottom: 3 0 0 5 1 3 3 3 2 0

WARSHIPS - 44

Right side: 1 4 0 2 3 1 3 2 4 0
Bottom: 1 2 3 0 1 6 1 1 5 0

WARSHIPS - 45

Right side: 3 3 0 2 2 1 3 2 4 0
Bottom: 3 0 4 0 1 4 1 4 3 0

WARSHIPS - 46

Right side: 1 2 2 3 2 0 2 4 0 4
Bottom: 1 1 3 0 3 2 3 2 5 0

WARSHIPS - 47

Right side: 1 0 3 3 2 4 2 3 1 1
Bottom: 4 0 5 1 0 4 2 2 2 0

WARSHIPS - 48

Right side: 0 5 1 1 2 1 5 1 4 0
Bottom: 1 3 1 3 4 1 0 6 0 1

CALCULDOKU

Calcudoku is played on a square grid. The most common Calcudoku grid sizes are between 4×4 and 9×9.

The object of the puzzle is to fill all the empty squares with the numbers 1 through X (where X is the grid size). Each number must appear once (and only once) in each column and each row.

For example, in a 4×4 Calcudoku puzzle, X is 4. This means the numbers 1, 2, 3, and 4 will appear once in each column and once in each row.

But wait! There's more (sorry, couldn't resist).

Every Calcudoku grid will have blocks in it that are surrounded by bolder lines. Each block will contain a result and math operator in its top-left corner. The numbers in the block must total the result using only the given operator. A number may be used more than once in the same block, as loing as it doesn't appear more than once per row/column.

GRID - 1

GRID - 2

GRID - 3

GRID - 4

GRID - 5

GRID - 6

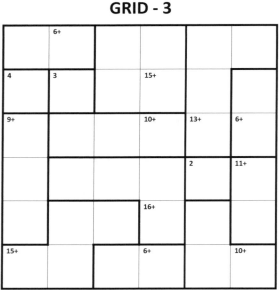

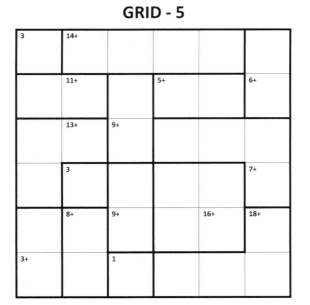

GRID - 7

6+	1			12+	6
	17+		1		7+
			8+		7+
				9+	
			10+		
15+	17+		10+		

GRID - 8

9+			2		3
	8+		9+		10+
6	15+				
7+					14+
	1	6+			8+
		11+			17+

GRID - 9

		7+	6+		2
17+					10+
	6+		11+	4+	
		4		6	5
5+	11+				
9+		9+		7+	7+

GRID - 10

5+	11+		6+		5
	12+				8+
					1
	3	4			11+
		11+	12+		
16+	6+				15+

GRID - 11

	8+	13+	7+		8+
			9+	6+	
5+		12+			
12+		6		3	15+
2	9+			11+	

GRID - 12

19+	6+		9+		12+
			5		
				2	
		10+		16+	6+
			5+	4	13+
6+	11+	2			

GRID - 13

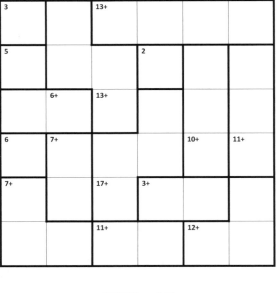

GRID - 14

GRID - 15

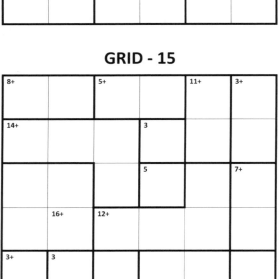

GRID - 16

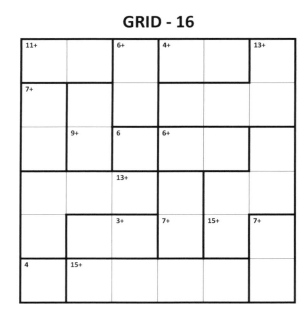

GRID - 17

GRID - 18

GRID - 19

	8+	7+			
	8+		12+	9+	
			4+		
7+	4	1	18+		15+
4+				8+	2
11+			5+		3

GRID - 20

	11+	9+	4	3	6+
12+					
	6+		18+		
		6		3+	5
	7+				17+
4+		8+	7+		

GRID - 21

	3	10+		5+	4+
	11+		8+		
15+			11+		6+
	11+	6			
			5+	5	11+
6+				9+	

GRID - 22

11+			3		13+
	13+		2		
					5
13+		5+	6+		
		12+		12+	9+
3		16+			3+

GRID - 23

	16+	7+		7+	
					8+
9+		6			
3	1		13+		
	5+				
		15+	9+	15+	12+

GRID - 24

15+				6+	5+
		7+			
			4	7+	
17+		9+	6	7+	1
12+			4+		6
10+				10+	

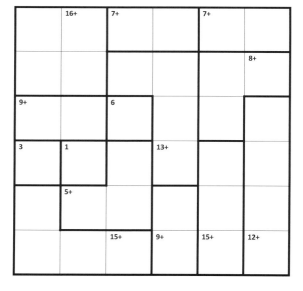

GRID - 25

GRID - 26

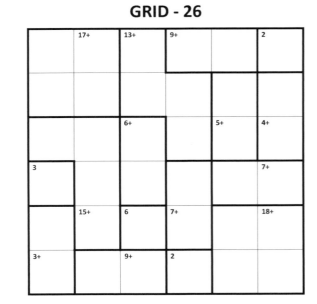

GRID - 27

GRID - 28

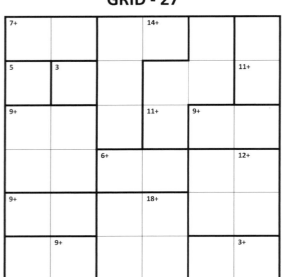

GRID - 29

GRID - 30

GRID - 31

	6+		3		17+
11+		4+	3+		
				1	
7+	4+	13+	18+		
12+		6			
			15+		6+

GRID - 32

7+	1	9+			15+
	8+				
1		5+	8+		
10+		16+	2		13+
15+				7+	
		2			7+

GRID - 33

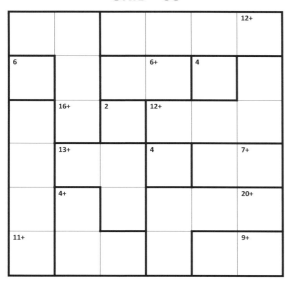

GRID - 34

		7+		6	7+
9+	4+			16+	
1	6			14+	
14+				10+	
	9+	16+	7+		

GRID - 35

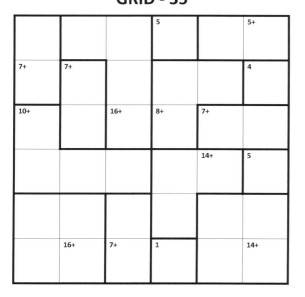

GRID - 36

	8+		9+		4+
	9+	11+			8+
4	6				
3+					18+
4+	3	6+			
		9+		14+	10+

GRID - 37

8+		9+		5+	
			4+	8+	
	18+	3	9+	2	1
3+		14+			8+
7+			15+		11+
		1			

GRID - 38

			16+		
					6+
15+	8+	10+			
1	7+			10+	11+
	15+		9+		3
		6+	8+		1

GRID - 39

	13+		7+		10+
8+	3				
16+				7+	
		13+	3		
		17+			
6+		6+	1	5	11+

GRID - 40

	6+	7+			
4	2	19+			12+
15+	7+		8+		
				11+	
		13+		5+	
			2	6	9+

GRID - 41

8+	12+		12+		
1	3			10+	
2	14+		4		18+
18+			6+		
		7+		8+	3+

GRID - 42

		16+	5+		
14+			4	3	8+
5+					10+
			6		
10+					8+
18+			12+	7+	

GRID - 43

11+					17+
14+			13+		3
	1		2		9+
				4+	
17+	3	12+			7+
				13+	

GRID - 44

6+		11+			11+
			11+		
7+	2			16+	5+
12+					13+
3		2		14+	
8+		5+			

GRID - 45

12+		12+			9+
	7+		3+		
	5				16+
	6		7+		
	6+		11+		6+
15+					11+

GRID - 46

8+				1	15+
		12+	7+	7+	
4+			13+	7+	4+
4	5				
5		7+		11+	
10+		6+			

GRID - 47

3	14+		7+		
					16+
3+	6	3			11+
	10+		3		14+
		3+	9+		
15+			9+		

GRID - 48

11+			9+		
8+				3+	5+
4+		8+	3		15+
	11+	5	2		
9+					
		3	11+	19+	

GRID - 49

9+			11+		8+
				6	3+
		7+		1	
13+		3+			8+
		3	17+		
7+	11+		3		16+

GRID - 50

			16+		
4+	17+				
10+		9+	6+	6+	1
	1	3			4
	6+			17+	9+
7+	10+				

GRID - 51

7+		5	9+		5+
9+		6+			
		15+			
				11+	8+
11+		10+	1		18+
			11+		

GRID - 52

					10+
	6+			14+	
14+					
18+	15+		14+	2	11+
		3+	7+		
		4	1	7+	

GRID - 53

					7+
	16+		5	15+	7+
13+			7+		
2			13+		
			8+		
9+	5	2		17+	

GRID - 54

		4			7+
8+	9+	3	11+		
2	4+	6+			7+
6					17+
	7+				
14+				13+	8+

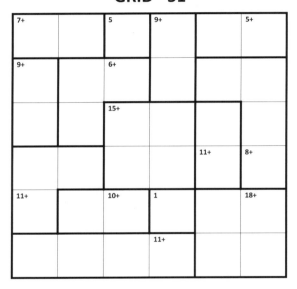

GRID - 55

14+			11+	
		6	2	
6+	6+			7+
			3	7+
	6+	14+	17+	
9+	9+		9+	

GRID - 56

17+				
2	15+	11+		9+
		9+		
	6		15+	
			6+	
13+	5+	2	5	11+

GRID - 57

4		8+		19+
3				
	12+	8+		
	12+		9+	13+
			5+	
14+	6	8+	5+	

GRID - 58

9+	11+			
	9+		2	16+
17+			5+	4
4+		10+	6	8+
	6+	7+	11+	1

GRID - 59

13+		4		11+
6+	4+	10+		
				3
	2	14+		
	10+		13+	20+
13+			3+	

GRID - 60

6+		13+	14+	
	4	9+	7+	
3				
10+		6	2	7+
	14+	13+		
3+		15+		

HOW TO PLAY

The game is typically played between two people.
- One person, the 'host' chooses a word and marks the length of the word on the grid.
- The other player has to guess the letters in this word/phrase before all the parts of the hangman are drawn,
- If the player guesses correctly the letter is marked in the correct place, if the player guesses incorrectly the host draws another part of the hangman,
- The game continues until
- the word/phrase is guessed (all letters are revealed) in this case the second person has won
- all the parts of the hangman are displayed in

Word: _____

| A B C D E F G H I J K L M N O |
| P Q R S T U V W X Y Z |

Word: _____

| A B C D E F G H I J K L M N O |
| P Q R S T U V W X Y Z |

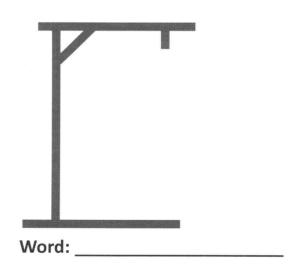

Word: _____

| A B C D E F G H I J K L M N O |
| P Q R S T U V W X Y Z |

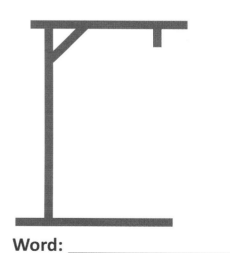

Word: _____

| A B C D E F G H I J K L M N O |
| P Q R S T U V W X Y Z |

Word: _____

ABCDEFGHIJKLMNO
PQRSTUVWXYZ

Word: _____

ABCDEFGHIJKLMNO
PQRSTUVWXYZ

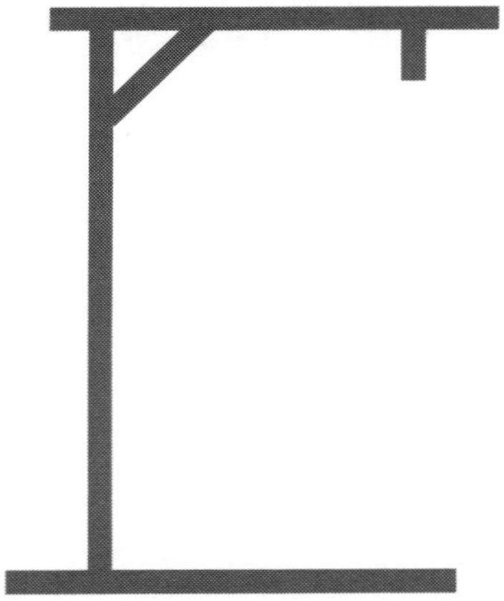

Word: _____

ABCDEFGHIJKLMNO
PQRSTUVWXYZ

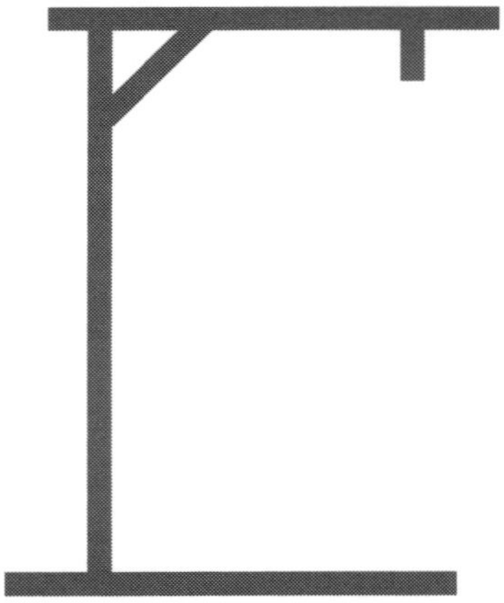

Word: _____

ABCDEFGHIJKLMNO
PQRSTUVWXYZ

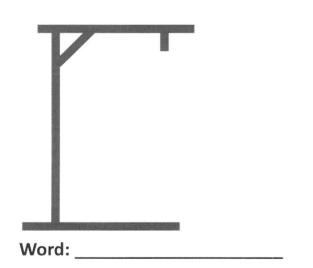

Word: _____

A B C D E F G H I J K L M N O
P Q R S T U V W X Y Z

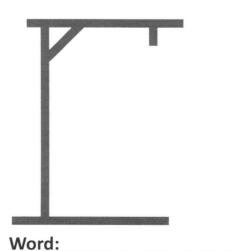

Word: _____

A B C D E F G H I J K L M N O
P Q R S T U V W X Y Z

Word: _____

A B C D E F G H I J K L M N O
P Q R S T U V W X Y Z

Word: _____

A B C D E F G H I J K L M N O
P Q R S T U V W X Y Z

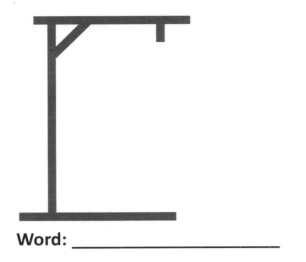

Word: _____

A B C D E F G H I J K L M N O P Q R S T U V W X Y Z	A B C D E F G H I J K L M N O P Q R S T U V W X Y Z

Word: _____

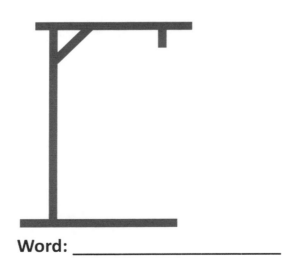

Word: _____

A B C D E F G H I J K L M N O P Q R S T U V W X Y Z	A B C D E F G H I J K L M N O P Q R S T U V W X Y Z

Word: _____

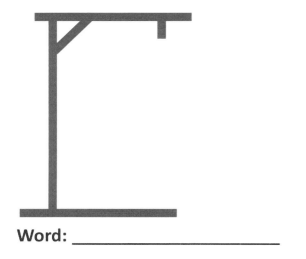

Word: _____

| A B C D E F G H I J K L M N O |
| P Q R S T U V W X Y Z |

Word: _____

| A B C D E F G H I J K L M N O |
| P Q R S T U V W X Y Z |

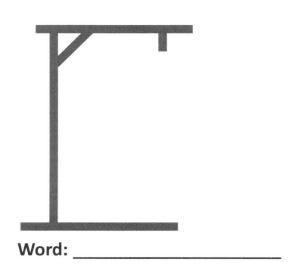

Word: _____

| A B C D E F G H I J K L M N O |
| P Q R S T U V W X Y Z |

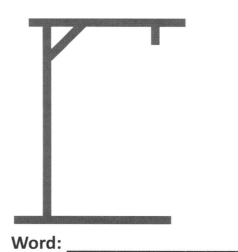

Word: _____

| A B C D E F G H I J K L M N O |
| P Q R S T U V W X Y Z |

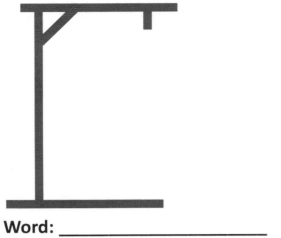

Word: _____

ABCDEFGHIJKLMNO
PQRSTUVWXYZ

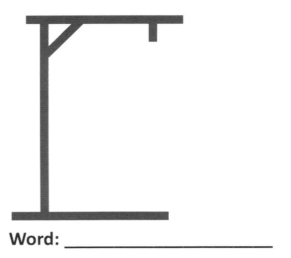

Word: _____

ABCDEFGHIJKLMNO
PQRSTUVWXYZ

Word: _____

ABCDEFGHIJKLMNO
PQRSTUVWXYZ

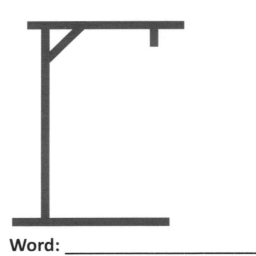

Word: _____

ABCDEFGHIJKLMNO
PQRSTUVWXYZ

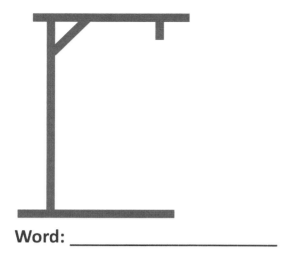

Word: _____

| A B C D E F G H I J K L M N O |
| P Q R S T U V W X Y Z |

Word: _____

| A B C D E F G H I J K L M N O |
| P Q R S T U V W X Y Z |

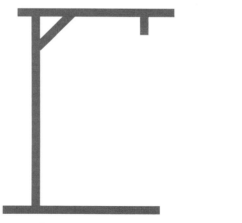

Word: _____

| A B C D E F G H I J K L M N O |
| P Q R S T U V W X Y Z |

Word: _____

| A B C D E F G H I J K L M N O |
| P Q R S T U V W X Y Z |

Word: _____

ABCDEFGHIJKLMNO
PQRSTUVWXYZ

Word: _____

ABCDEFGHIJKLMNO
PQRSTUVWXYZ

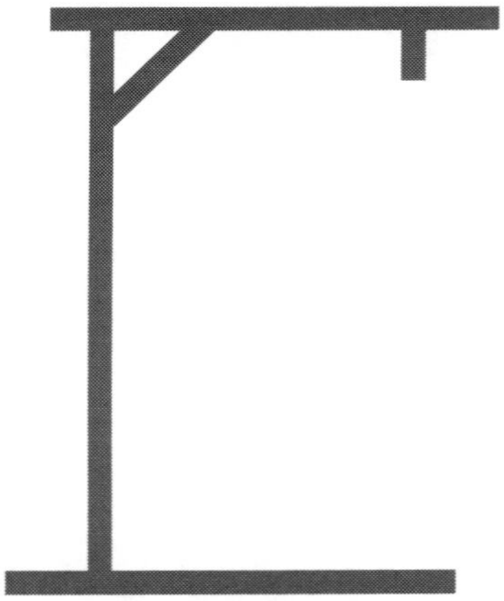

Word: _____

ABCDEFGHIJKLMNO
PQRSTUVWXYZ

Word: _____

ABCDEFGHIJKLMNO
PQRSTUVWXYZ

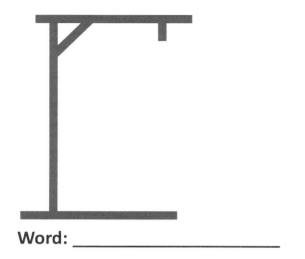

Word: _____

| A B C D E F G H I J K L M N O |
| P Q R S T U V W X Y Z |

Word: _____

| A B C D E F G H I J K L M N O |
| P Q R S T U V W X Y Z |

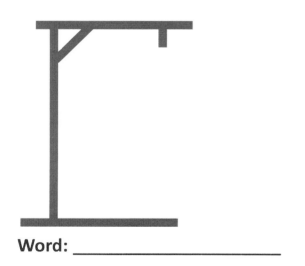

Word: _____

| A B C D E F G H I J K L M N O |
| P Q R S T U V W X Y Z |

Word: _____

| A B C D E F G H I J K L M N O |
| P Q R S T U V W X Y Z |

Word: _____

ABCDEFGHIJKLMNO
PQRSTUVWXYZ

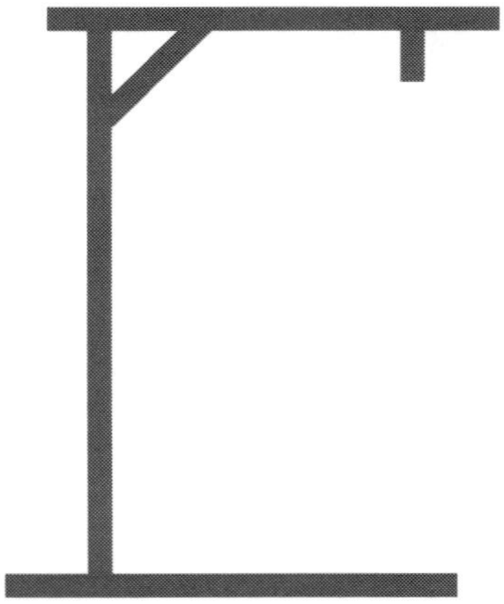

Word: _____

ABCDEFGHIJKLMNO
PQRSTUVWXYZ

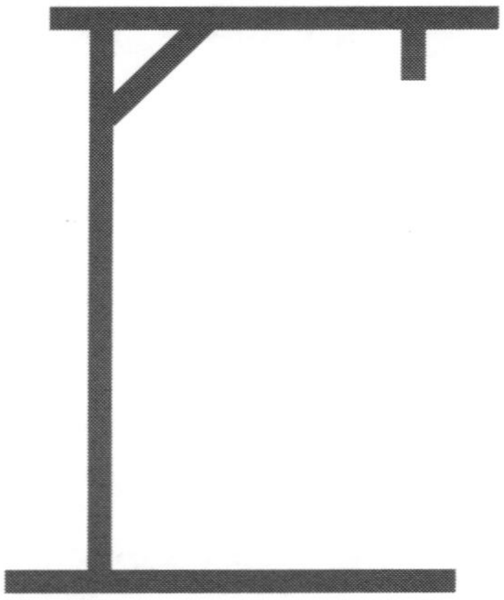

Word: _____

ABCDEFGHIJKLMNO
PQRSTUVWXYZ

Word: _____

ABCDEFGHIJKLMNO
PQRSTUVWXYZ

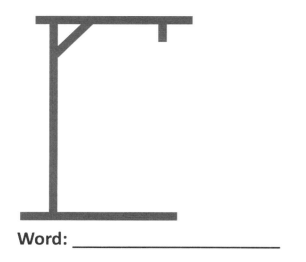

Word: _____

| A B C D E F G H I J K L M N O |
| P Q R S T U V W X Y Z |

Word: _____

| A B C D E F G H I J K L M N O |
| P Q R S T U V W X Y Z |

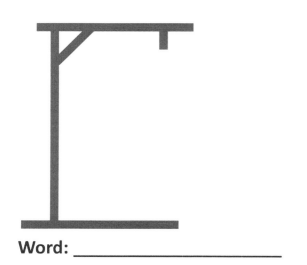

Word: _____

| A B C D E F G H I J K L M N O |
| P Q R S T U V W X Y Z |

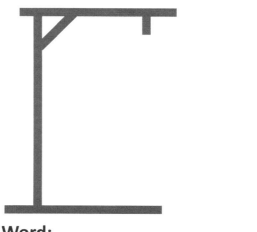

Word: _____

| A B C D E F G H I J K L M N O |
| P Q R S T U V W X Y Z |

Word: _____

ABCDEFGHIJKLMNO
PQRSTUVWXYZ

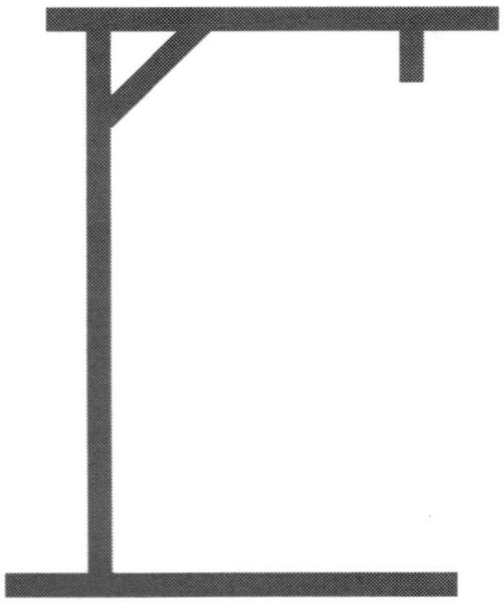

Word: _____

ABCDEFGHIJKLMNO
PQRSTUVWXYZ

Word: _____

ABCDEFGHIJKLMNO
PQRSTUVWXYZ

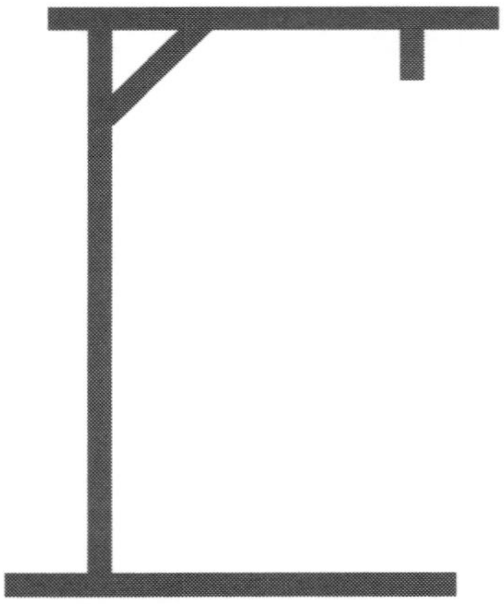

Word: _____

ABCDEFGHIJKLMNO
PQRSTUVWXYZ

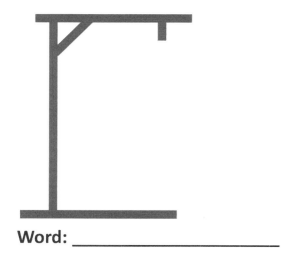

Word: _____

A B C D E F G H I J K L M N O
P Q R S T U V W X Y Z

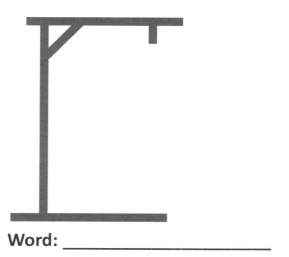

Word: _____

A B C D E F G H I J K L M N O
P Q R S T U V W X Y Z

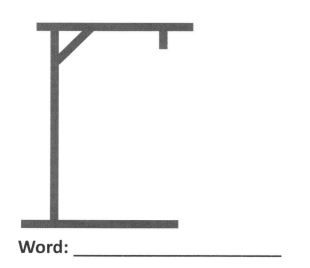

Word: _____

A B C D E F G H I J K L M N O
P Q R S T U V W X Y Z

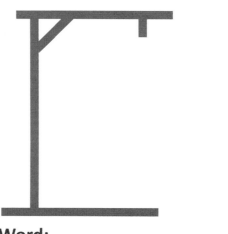

Word: _____

A B C D E F G H I J K L M N O
P Q R S T U V W X Y Z

Word: _____

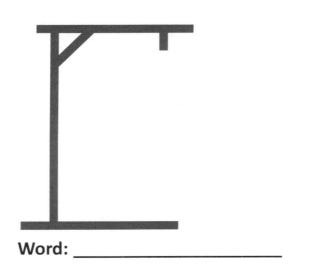

| A B C D E F G H I J K L M N O |
| P Q R S T U V W X Y Z |

Word: _____

| A B C D E F G H I J K L M N O |
| P Q R S T U V W X Y Z |

Word: _____

| A B C D E F G H I J K L M N O |
| P Q R S T U V W X Y Z |

Word: _____

| A B C D E F G H I J K L M N O |
| P Q R S T U V W X Y Z |

Word: _____

```
A B C D E F G H I J K L M N O
P Q R S T U V W X Y Z
```

Word: _____

```
A B C D E F G H I J K L M N O
P Q R S T U V W X Y Z
```

Word: _____

```
A B C D E F G H I J K L M N O
P Q R S T U V W X Y Z
```

Word: _____

```
A B C D E F G H I J K L M N O
P Q R S T U V W X Y Z
```

Word: _____

```
A B C D E F G H I J K L M N O
P Q R S T U V W X Y Z
```

Word: _____

```
A B C D E F G H I J K L M N O
P Q R S T U V W X Y Z
```

Word: _____

```
A B C D E F G H I J K L M N O
P Q R S T U V W X Y Z
```

Word: _____

```
A B C D E F G H I J K L M N O
P Q R S T U V W X Y Z
```

Word: _____

```
A B C D E F G H I J K L M N O
P Q R S T U V W X Y Z
```

Word: _____

```
A B C D E F G H I J K L M N O
P Q R S T U V W X Y Z
```

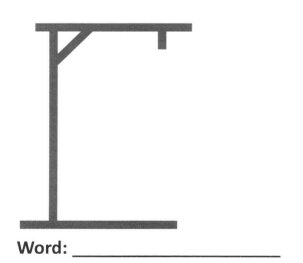

Word: _____

```
A B C D E F G H I J K L M N O
P Q R S T U V W X Y Z
```

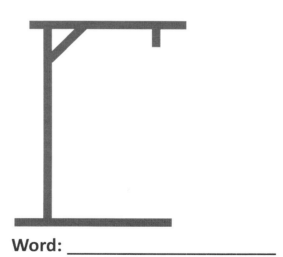

Word: _____

```
A B C D E F G H I J K L M N O
P Q R S T U V W X Y Z
```

Word: _____

| A B C D E F G H I J K L M N O |
| P Q R S T U V W X Y Z |

Word: _____

| A B C D E F G H I J K L M N O |
| P Q R S T U V W X Y Z |

Word: _____

| A B C D E F G H I J K L M N O |
| P Q R S T U V W X Y Z |

Word: _____

| A B C D E F G H I J K L M N O |
| P Q R S T U V W X Y Z |

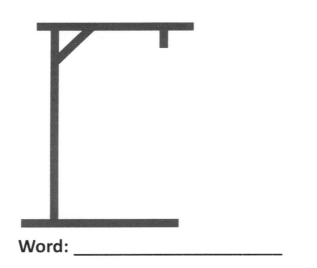

HOW TO PLAY

Sudoku is played on a grid of 9 x 9 spaces. Within the rows and columns are 9 "squares" (made up of 3 x 3 spaces). Each row, column and square (9 spaces each) needs to be filled out with the numbers 1-9, without repeating any numbers within the row, column or square. Does it sound complicated? As you can see from the image below of an actual Sudoku grid, each Sudoku grid comes with a few spaces already filled in; the more spaces filled in, the easier the game – the more difficult Sudoku puzzles have very few spaces that are already filled in.

SUDOKU - 1

6		8		9		4	5	
9	5		1		4	8		
2	3					9		
	2	6		1	3		8	4
4	8		5					
7			4	2		5	6	
	4	5					9	
	6		8	4		2		
8		2				3	4	

SUDOKU - 2

1				9			3	
3			8			5	4	2
		5		4				9
	6				3	2		
5		2	4					3
4		3		2			5	7
9	5			3	8	4		1
2	4		9	6		3	8	5
8		1		7	4			6

SUDOKU - 3

			8	5	1	7	4	
				4	2	9		8
	1		6			3		5
7	6	1		3				2
8	2	5	1			6		9
9		3	2	8	6		5	
5			9			8		
		6	4		8			
				6				3

SUDOKU - 4

		2		6	3	8		4
6	1	4	8	2			5	
			5	4				
4		1		5				6
	5	3						
8		9			1	3		
	6	7	1	5			8	
2			9		6		4	5
1				4			6	3

SUDOKU - 5

				4				
			8	1		5	9	
9	4	2		5				3
	6	4	2	3				7
2		5	9	6		3		8
	8	9		7		2	1	6
7	9	8	5	2			3	
			7			6		9
	2				3			

SUDOKU - 6

3	6			9	4		2	
					7			
9	7		3			6	1	
	2		1			8	4	9
				7	2		1	
5	1		4	6				8
7		5			1	6	3	
		8		3	9		5	1
1	3						8	4

4

SUDOKU - 7

		9	2	3	6	4	8	
	3	2	1		7			5
		6		9	4	3	2	1
5	4		7					
				3	8			9
	9						5	4
8	7					1	9	
9		5						3
6		3		4	2	5		

SUDOKU - 8

8				4			5	
4	3	9		2		1	6	8
7			6	3		4		2
			9	1			8	
1		4	8			5	3	
			3		7	2		4
	4				1			3
5		7				6		
		1		4		6	8	2

SUDOKU - 9

				5	2	6		
6	2		9	1			7	4
5		1	6	4	7	8	2	
4			1	8				6
		9	5	2	4	1		
	1				9	2	4	5
9	8			7				
	7						5	1
1					5			

SUDOKU - 10

2			8		4		3	7
8			5			6		
4			2			8		1
	9	1	6		8			5
			7	2		3		9
3		2	9		1			8
	2		3	5		1		4
	6				2		9	3
5				9				6

SUDOKU - 11

		9		2			4	6
		6	1		5	7	2	
7	2					3	8	
	3	1			2			
9		2		8		6	3	
5			8	3			9	
2				5	7			
8	6			1		9	5	
	5			9			6	7

SUDOKU - 12

		7	1				8	9
	1				7	6		4
	6	4	5	8	9	2	7	1
	9			3			1	7
		3			5			
	7	2				8	9	3
	2						4	5
		5	9		8			
9	3			5		7	6	

5

SUDOKU - 13

		7		4		9		
4	3		1			2		5
	6		7		5		1	3
		1	2		8			9
8						3		
	5	9		6	1	8		7
	4	6		5	3		9	
7				2		1	5	
	8	5			7			4

SUDOKU - 14

	3	9	2			4	1	
	5			6		9		7
6		2		4	1		3	8
			4		2			
3	6	1		7				
4			3		5			
		6				4		7
2	1			9	8	6	4	5
7				2		8	9	

SUDOKU - 15

2		5			4		7	6
	3		5			4		
7	6				9	3		
	4			1				2
3		2				8		
5			8	4		7	9	
						3	6	5
4	7	3	6	5			2	9
6	5		3		8	4	1	7

SUDOKU - 16

		1	7			3		
				4				
	8		3	6	9		4	
4	6			7		5		3
8		9		5			2	
7		3	6	8	2			
1				7		8		2
9	2		8	4	6	7		1
6	7					9	5	

SUDOKU - 17

	8	1	3			6	2	4
7	9		1					3
	4	3	8				1	
	5		4		2	7	9	
		8			6			
	1	4		7	8			
		7		4			6	5
4	6		7			1	2	3
8	2	9	6		3			

SUDOKU - 18

			1	2				
	6	2	4		3		8	
5		1		8	6	4	2	
2			3					5
7			6		2	3		
	8			9			6	
3	9	8		6			4	7
	1	5	7			8		
4			8	3	5		9	

SUDOKU - 19

		9		4	5		8	
2	7	1			8		6	5
4				2			9	3
5		4	2	7	3		1	
	2				1		7	
			8	9			3	2
			5		7			9
9	1	3				2	7	
7		2			9	8		1

SUDOKU - 20

				1	4	7		
4	7					6	2	
	3				6	9	8	4
1	8		4					
	4		3	9	8		1	
	9	5		6		8		
9		8	2	3			6	
2	6	3	5					
7					1	2	3	9

SUDOKU - 21

2	1	7		5	9	8	4	3
			1	7		2		9
9		5	2	8				7
6	2						8	
7				9				
			8	4	6			1
	9	2		3	8	5		
		3	9			4	7	2
	7					9		

SUDOKU - 22

7		6	5				8	
	8	2	1		6			
3	5		2	4				
2	9	5	8	1			6	7
		8		5	9		2	
	3		6	2	7			8
5	2						4	
	4			8		6	5	1
8					5			

SUDOKU - 23

3	6						1	2
		5		2				
8					6			
2			4	7	3	9	6	
			8	1	5			
	3	4	2			7	8	1
7					6	2	4	
4		8	7	5	2	1	3	6
		6	3	9	4			

SUDOKU - 24

			9					
			7		6	1		2
	6			5		3	7	9
		8	5	9				4
2	7	6						8
9	4	1	6	3	8		2	7
4	9	3	8			2	5	1
						7	8	3
		8	1	2				

SUDOKU - 25

7			1	9				
	1	4				2		
	3				4	8	1	
		8	5	4	7			9
	5	3		2	1	7	6	4
			9			1	8	5
		5	4	6				1
	9	1				4	3	
2	4		3			6		

SUDOKU - 26

			9	4	2			
7							1	
4	3		7					6
9	6				7		4	8
	7	8	6	9		5	3	
5		2			3			
8	1	7	2			4		
	5		1	3	8			7
		6			5	8	2	1

SUDOKU - 27

9	4	8					2	5
5		2		4			7	
7		6	5	3				
	5		7			6		
6	7		3	2	5	9	8	4
		4						3
			2	9	8			1
				6		8		
1	8		4	5	7	2		

SUDOKU - 28

		1				9		
3		2			5		6	1
							5	
1	9		4			6		5
	3	6	5	9	8		1	
	2		3		6			
6	7				3		9	2
8			2	6	7	5		
2		3		4	9	1	7	

SUDOKU - 29

5	6				1	7		
	1		5	3	7			2
3			4	6		9		
7		1	8	9	4		2	
8		9	6		2		5	7
					5			
2		7				6		
				4	9		7	3
	9		7	5	6		8	

SUDOKU - 30

8	4	9	1				2	
5	1			9				
		6	2	3	8	4	9	
6	8		7			1	3	2
	2	7			9	1		8
		3		8	2		5	
	9		4					
3	5				1		4	7
		4	9		5			

SUDOKU - 31

6			7	4	5	9	2	
						1	8	
3	5							7
		5				2	6	9
4			3	2				8
	1	8		5		7		
8	9	6	4	7	1			2
	7	4	2	6	3	8	9	
1			5	8				

SUDOKU - 32

2	4	6	7	5	8	3		
1	9		4				2	8
				1	7			4
	5	1						
4	3		5			2		7
7				1				6
8		3			5			
		4	8	3	2		7	
		2	6		7	9		3

SUDOKU - 33

9	3		7		1			
5	2			4	6	9	1	
1	6	7		9			4	
3		1	4	8				
		9				5	7	
4	7	2		6	5			
7	9		2	1			5	
2						8	9	
8	4	6				7		

SUDOKU - 34

4	5	6		3				
7	9		5		6	3		1
	3	2				5		7
			3	1				8
		1	7		4	2		
2			8			9	1	
			6	5	3		2	
5	2		9			6		
6		9			8	1		5

SUDOKU - 35

			1	7	3			2
3				8		9	6	
2	8	1	4	6	9		3	
9		6						3
1			3					9
7		8		9	1	5	4	
4	9	3	7		2	6		
	2	7				1		
				6			2	

SUDOKU - 36

	2		3	6	4			1
		9	5		7	3		
	6	1		9			4	5
5			9				7	8
		6			5	1		
			8			5		9
	4	7			8		5	3
		8		4		6		
	3		6	5		4	8	7

SUDOKU - 37

	4	9			7		8	3
				4		7		1
				8	6	4		2
						6		5
	6	8	4	5	9			7
5	2	4						9
	5	6	1	9	2		7	8
7	9			3	8	2		
8		2						

SUDOKU - 38

			2		1		9	3
6	1	3	7	5		2	8	
		9		3			1	
					3		4	6
8				4	2			9
	5	4		7		1	3	
				1	6			8
1	4		3	8	7		6	
	6		9			5	4	

SUDOKU - 39

					8	7		9
2	7	4	9		6			
9								2
5	2	6	3	4	9		8	7
7			8	5	6			
3	9			1			5	
	3	9	1		2		7	5
1						4		
			7	5	4		3	

SUDOKU - 40

9		6			5	4	2	
5	7			8			9	3
4			3				5	1
2	5				8	9		
3	6			2	7		1	5
		8						2
8		5		6	9	1		
6			8	7			4	9
		9						6

SUDOKU - 41

2	1							
		4	2	1	8	3	7	
	9		3	5	4			2
8	5	2					4	3
			5	2	9	8	1	7
1	7	9	4	8		5	2	6
3			6	4				
								5
		5	1					

SUDOKU - 42

3				7				
	4		2		3	1	5	
			6			3	8	
6		1	3			5	9	4
9				6		7		
2	7	5	9		4	6	3	8
	2		7	3	8		1	
8			5				6	3
	3					8		

10

	7	4	6	5		9		1
2			8	1		4	7	3
9			3	7	4		2	
	3	5			8	1		9
6			7					
	1					3	4	7
1		8						
		3		8				5
		7		2	3	8	9	

	6		1	4	7	8		5
5		9					7	4
7		1		8		2		6
3		7		1			8	2
	9	4				5		
6	2	8				4		7
			8			6		
	7		5			3		8
	1			6		7	4	

	4	2	6			1		
1	9	3		4		8		
6		5	2		1		7	
2		1	9		4		3	8
9		4		3		7	6	
		8	5		7		4	
5		6	1					2
8					6		1	
					8			7

4	5	2					1	7
8	7		5		2	4		6
9	6		4	1		5	8	
	9				6	7		
	2				9		6	5
	4		3		1	8		9
			7			5		
2	8			9				
7	1			2	3			

5	9		4	3	8			7
	2	3		9		1	4	
	8	6	2			5		
8			9	1			2	3
	1	2	8	4		9	7	
		9			7			4
	3		1		2		8	
1			3			7		
		8	7		9		5	

4	7		6		1			
6	8	2	9	5	7		3	
				2		6		
		3	5			1		
	1			2	9			5
				1	4	9		3
		6	4		3	8		
1	4		2	8	5			
	2			9	6		4	7

SUDOKU - 49

```
. . . | 4 . . | . . 5
5 . . | . 9 . | . . .
. . 1 | 3 . 7 | . . .
------+-------+------
9 6 2 | . . 4 | . 5 .
7 . . | . 6 5 | 1 4 2
1 . 4 | . 8 3 | 9 7 .
------+-------+------
3 1 . | 8 . . | 4 6 .
. 2 9 | . 3 . | . 8 7
6 . 8 | . . 9 | . 2 .
```

SUDOKU - 50

```
7 . . | . . . | . 3 .
8 9 . | 3 4 . | . 7 1
3 . . | . . 2 | 6 8 4
------+-------+------
. 6 8 | 7 . . | 1 . 9
. . . | . . 6 | 7 . 8
5 4 7 | 1 8 . | 3 . .
------+-------+------
. 7 . | 5 2 1 | . . 3
. . 2 | 4 . . | . 9 7
. . 3 | . 9 . | . . 2
```

SUDOKU - 51

```
. . 7 | . . . | 3 . .
6 8 4 | 2 . . | 5 . .
. . . | 6 5 . | . 2 4
------+-------+------
2 4 8 | 7 1 . | 6 5 9
. . . | 4 . 6 | 2 . 8
. 9 . | 5 . 8 | . 4 7
------+-------+------
4 . 1 | . . . | 7 . .
. 3 2 | 8 . . | 9 6 .
. 6 . | . 7 . | . . .
```

SUDOKU - 52

```
. . . | 3 9 5 | . . 1
. 7 . | . 6 . | 4 . 8
. . . | . . . | . . 3
------+-------+------
1 . 6 | 4 9 . | 2 8 7
. 5 2 | 3 8 7 | 9 1 6
. . . | 2 6 3 | . . 4
------+-------+------
6 2 . | 8 . . | . . .
. . 4 | . 1 . | . . .
. 1 3 | . . 4 | 8 7 .
```

SUDOKU - 53

```
3 1 . | . . . | . . .
2 7 . | . . 9 | . 5 6
. . 6 | . 7 . | 3 9 .
------+-------+------
4 . 5 | . 1 8 | . 2 9
7 . . | 5 9 . | 8 . 3
. 8 . | . 4 7 | 5 6 1
------+-------+------
. 9 3 | . 5 . | . . 4
. 2 . | . . . | . . 5
. . 8 | . . 1 | . 3 7
```

SUDOKU - 54

```
. . . | . . . | . 9 .
. 7 4 | 6 3 . | 1 8 .
. 5 8 | 7 9 . | . . 4
------+-------+------
. 6 2 | . 5 7 | 3 1 .
. . . | 8 1 6 | 5 . .
7 . 5 | . 2 3 | . 6 .
------+-------+------
5 . . | . . 9 | 8 4 .
. 4 6 | . . . | 9 . 3
. . . | . . . | 6 5 1
```

SUDOKU - 55

	3	6		2	7			
1		7	3		4	8		
	9	5				3		
	1		7	4	5	6		
	5			3		7		1
					6	5		8
3		9	4	5	2	1		
5					8	2	6	
	8		1			4	9	

SUDOKU - 56

	5		9				1	7
4	8				3			
		1	9		4		5	3
	4	1	2			3	8	6
7	6	5	8		4	9		2
	3			9		7		
	7			2				3
				8	1			
	9		3	5	7	6		

SUDOKU - 57

6				9	2		8	7
	8	2	3			6		
	5	7	8		1		2	3
			9	2				6
	6			5			4	
	9	5		1			7	
5		9						8
7			1		8	3	9	
		8	2	5	9	7		

SUDOKU - 58

			9	8	5	6	1	4
				7		3		2
			2					9
9	7	8		2				1
3	1	5	4		7	2	9	8
6	2	4	8	1	9		5	3
	6		3					
	4	2			8			
								7

SUDOKU - 59

		7	6	9	3			
3			4				8	1
9		2		5	8			
		9	7	4			1	2
7			2		6	3		9
	2		3	1	9	6	7	
4			8	6		1		
			9	3			4	8
		1	5		4			6

SUDOKU - 60

					1	6		
	7	6	5		9			2
8		9		4			3	5
	6	3	8		7		5	
9	2		4	1	6	8		
	8	7		2				
	3	1	2		8		6	4
						3		7
			9	6	3	5		

SUDOKU - 61

4				8		3		
			4	9	7	2		5
9	8	7				4		
1	4		6	5	3	8		
	6			2	9	1		4
	2	5	8			9		3
2				6	5			
8				4	1			2
		4	2			6	9	

SUDOKU - 62

6	1		9	5		3		
3						9	4	
2		9		7	3	6		5
	2		4	6	9		3	
9	3			8		1	6	
	6			1			2	
	7			9		2		
1		6	8				5	
5	8	2		3	1		9	

SUDOKU - 63

6		8		5	7		9	
1			8	9			6	
		3	2				7	8
9		5			8	6		7
			9	7		8	1	4
7			3				5	2
2	5			8	9			1
8			5	4	1		2	
4				3				6

SUDOKU - 64

3	4	6		5			8	
5	8	1	9	2				3
7			4			1		
1	2	9					3	
8	5		2			6	7	
		7		1		5		2
	1					9	2	8
9		5	6			4		
				4			5	6

SUDOKU - 65

2	1	5						
7	3	9	5		1	6	8	
							2	
			8	7	5			
		4				2		
1				9	2	8		
	2		9	8	4		5	7
8	4	7		5		9		2
		5		2	1	7	4	6

SUDOKU - 66

6			8		9		5	
		8			5			7
4							1	
		3		2		9		
				6	1		8	5
9				5	8		2	4
1	4	2		9	3	5	7	
3		9	5	1	7	2		
	7			8	2			3

14

SUDOKU - 67

8		2				4		3
6	3				4			
4	1			3		6		5
	6	4		7			5	
1	9		5	8			6	
2			4		6	1		
9			8	4			1	
5	4				9	7		
7		6		5	1	3		

SUDOKU - 68

				8		1	3	
4	6	3	7	5	1			
	1	8	9		2		6	7
1		7	5		6	2		
			3					1
2	5	6	1				7	
			2				9	
7	4		8		3		2	
6		5	4			8		

SUDOKU - 69

2	5		6		7			8
4			5	8		9		
	3	9	1		4		7	
1		5	7	4	3			6
			2		1		3	7
		6		8		4		
5		3	4	1				9
			8		5			
6	1	4			2			

SUDOKU - 70

		3			7	6	9	
	9		3		5	2	8	7
			8	9			5	3
2		5	9				3	
3	7		5		2			6
			3	8		7		
	5	2			3			
			2	9		8		
	4	9	7			3	2	1

SUDOKU - 71

1	5				9	4	6	
				5		7		
6		7				8	5	
			6	7	3			9
	1	9		3	8	2		6
	3		2	9			1	8
			7		3	6		4
		3		4	2		5	
	7		6				3	2

SUDOKU - 72

	6		9	8				2
			5			9		4
		7		6	2		8	
6		5					1	7
1				8				
9		8		1		4	2	3
		6		3			7	9
4		2		7		1		8
		9	8		5	3	4	6

15

CROSSWORD

Would you like to improve your vocabulary, learn interesting new facts, and enhance your critical thinking skills? Solving crossword puzzles may be the answer! Crossword puzzles are complex word puzzles that are enjoyable, relaxing, and rewarding. This guide will share some information about crossword puzzles and how they are completed.

Crossword puzzles are drawn puzzles that are usually in the shape of a square or rectangle. The puzzle is filled with black and white squares. The goal of a crossword puzzle is to fill the white boxes with the answers to a series of questions. Most crosswords include numbers in the white squares so the player can match each question with a specific answer location. The shaded squares are used to separate the answers.

CROSSWORD Puzzle : 1

1	2	3	4		5	6	7	8		9	10	11

ACROSS
1. Fat
5. Small particle
9. - Guevara
12. Hip bones
13. Solitary
14. Utterance of hesitation
15. Wanes
16. Beer (Colloq)
17. Freeze
18. Monetary unit of China
20. Wine shelves
22. Character
25. Transfix
26. Long (for)
27. Hazy
28. Exclamation of surprise
31. Sea eagle
32. Item of headwear
33. Dossier
34. To clothe
35. City in NW Iran
36. Senior
37. Public transport
38. Halted briefly

39. Person hiring
42. Gentle
43. Revised form of Esperanto
44. 12th month of the Jewish calendar
46. Small island
50. Apex
51. Never
52. Dot
53. Wily
54. Exchange
55. Good-bye (2-2)

DOWN
1. Falsehood
2. Long-sleeved linen vestment
3. Chest bone
4. Carnivorous marsupial
5. Pond scum
6. Ripped
7. Yoko -
8. Caprice
9. Stylish
10. Cut ruthlessly
11. Female sheep

19. Vase
21. Prefix meaning without
22. Russian no
23. Prefix, air
24. Sharp taste
25. Fruit seed
27. Weir
28. Helps
29. To the sheltered side
30. Flock of cattle
32. Long-leaved lettuce
33. Flute player
35. Monarchs
36. Clumsy person
37. To exist
38. Coral builder
39. Strikes
40. Object of worship
41. Resembling a rope
42. Chapter of the Koran
45. Statute
47. Mineral spring
48. Auction item
49. Greek letter

CROSSWORD Puzzle : 2

ACROSS
1. Fumelike
5. Roster
9. Once common, now banned, insecticide
12. Son of Isaac and Rebekah
13. Personalities
14. Acknowledgement of debt
15. Building side
16. Ethereal
17. Gist
18. A Great Lake
20. Lord
22. Monetary unit
25. Bread roll
26. Jargon
27. Thrash
28. Lad
31. Music synthesiser
32. Musical instrument
33. Transport ticket cost
34. Sea eagle
35. Slack
36. Metropolitan
37. Family
38. Court cases
39. Outer coat of a seed
42. First class (1-3)
43. Room within a harem
44. Face cover
46. Cosy corner
50. Leg
51. Opera solo
52. Cube
53. Electrical unit
54. Remain
55. Metal dross

DOWN
1. Not many
2. America (Abbr)
3. - de mer, seasickness
4. Christmas log
5. Ventilate again
6. Double curve
7. Rocky peak
8. Sanctuary
9. Eat
10. Cricketer, - Walters
11. Pipe
19. Male sheep
21. Prefix meaning not
22. American coin
23. Scent
24. King of the beasts
25. Evil
27. Unit of illumination
28. Small yeast cake
29. Spoken
30. Desires
32. Large tree
33. Companions
35. South American beasts
36. Vase
37. Neuter singular pronoun
38. Hungarian wine
39. Roman garment
40. Dutch cheese
41. Coarsely ground corn
42. Largest continent
45. Talent
47. Lubricant
48. Wood sorrel
49. Beer barrel

CROSSWORD Puzzle : 3

1	2	3	4		5	6	7	8		9	10	11
12					13					14		
15					16					17		
			18	19				20	21			
22	23	24				25						
26					27				28	29	30	
31				32				33				
34				35			36					
		37				38						
39	40	41			42							
43			44	45				46	47	48	49	
50			51				52					
53			54				55					

ACROSS
1. Lacelike
5. Empty
9. Castrated male cat
12. Pain
13. River in central Switzerland
14. Card game
15. Ale
16. Fertiliser
17. Sexless things
18. Long fish
20. Havana resident
22. Necktie
25. Policeman
26. Capital of Morocco
27. Prefix, not
28. Dance step
31. Level
32. Kinsman
33. Cult
34. Conger
35. Drinking vessel
36. Keyboard instrument
37. Needlefish
38. Xmas tree decoration

39. A jewel
42. Tier
43. Room within a harem
44. Gloomy
46. Wyatt -
50. To date
51. The maple
52. Lion's call
53. Cracker biscuit
54. Refined woman
55. Inner Hebrides island

DOWN
1. Laboratory
2. Top card
3. - Guevara
4. Capital of Armenia
5. Crypt
6. Paddles
7. Anger
8. Church officer
9. Voluble
10. Jot
11. Boatswain
19. Consume

21. Toward the top
22. American Indian
23. Rant
24. Cain's victim
25. Corn ear
27. Pinch
28. Legumes
29. Adolescent pimples
30. Short take-off and landing
    aircraft
32. Prefix, over
33. Fishing weights
35. Taillike
36. Transfix
37. Depart
38. Loiter
39. Lads
40. Notion
41. Jet-assisted takeoff
42. Regretted
45. Wood sorrel
47. Very good (1-2)
48. Sunbeam
49. Prefix, before

CROSSWORD Puzzle : 4

1	2	3	4		5	6	7	8		9	10	11
12					13					14		
15					16					17		
			18	19				20	21			
22	23	24					25					
26					27					28	29	30
31				32				33				
34				35				36				
			37				38					
39	40	41				42						
43				44	45				46	47	48	49
50				51					52			
53				54					55			

ACROSS
1. Swine
5. Annoys
9. State of drowsy contentment
12. European mountain range
13. Metal spike
14. Room within a harem
15. Verne's submariner
16. Upswept hairdo
17. Sharp projection
18. Delay
20. Moves in water
22. Aver
25. Definite article
26. Entertain
27. No
28. Handwoven Scandinavian rug
31. Small animal
32. Acknowledgement of debt
33. Sound of a cat
34. Ovum
35. Auction item
36. Tint
37. French, good
38. Derived from a halogen

39. Athlete's foot
42. Put to sea
43. Bullfight call
44. Notes at scale's ends
46. Sicilian volcano
50. An evergreen
51. Black
52. Lion's call
53. A craze
54. Uproar
55. Stalk

DOWN
1. Play on words
2. Anger
3. Leg
4. Most sluggish
5. Eskimo
6. Ecstatic
7. Young goat
8. Sloppy
9. Fungus used in making soy sauce
10. Dutch cheese
11. Tires
19. Land measure

21. Plural of I
22. River in central Switzerland
23. Complacent
24. Carolled
25. Greek letter
27. Negating word
28. U.S. divorce city
29. Practitioner of yoga
30. Overwhelmed
32. Charged particle
33. Grain grinders
35. Machine that loads
36. - Chi. Slow moving martial art
   form
37. To exist
38. Contraction of has not
39. Dandy
40. Hip bones
41. Dweeb
42. Begone
45. Japanese sash
47. Young child
48. Not
49. Limb

CROSSWORD Puzzle : 5

1	2	3	4		5	6	7	8		9	10	11
12					13					14		
15					16					17		
			18	19				20	21			
22	23	24					25					
26						27				28	29	30
31					32				33			
34				35				36				
			37				38					
39	40	41				42						
43				44	45				46	47	48	49
50				51					52			
53				54					55			

ACROSS
1. Arm extremity
5. Talking bird
9. Eccentric wheel
12. 8th month of the Jewish calendar
13. Great age
14. Wood sorrel
15. Prefix, part
16. Cloistered women
17. Greek letter
18. Soak up sun
20. Rouse from sleep
22. Dismal
25. Scottish hill
26. Marine mammal
27. Jolt
28. Revised form of Esperanto
31. Assistant
32. Spoil
33. Songbird
34. "The Raven" author
35. Doomed
36. Suborn
37. Mate
38. Brags

39. Chinese
42. Groan
43. I have
44. Holly
46. Strong wind
50. Zero
51. Cut with laser
52. Willing
53. Wily
54. Nestling
55. Send out

DOWN
1. Belonging to him
2. Affirmative vote
3. Vietnam
4. Slobber
5. Ecclesiastical residence
6. Itch
7. Prefix, not
8. Reply
9. Rooster
10. Pain
11. Chief
19. Land measure

21. Prefix meaning without
22. Exchange
23. U.S. State
24. Compelled
25. Metal rod
27. Mischievous bird
28. Eye part
29. Something owing
30. Single items
32. Actor, - Gibson
33. Argue
35. Fluent
36. Large snake
37. The ratio between circumference
    and diameter
38. Crates
39. Transgressions
40. Sinister
41. Depend
42. Rocky tableland
45. Secular
47. Intention
48. Garland
49. Newt

CROSSWORD Puzzle : 6

ACROSS
1. Weeps
5. Munch
9. Witness
12. Envelop
13. Tempt
14. High-pitched
15. Abominable snowman
16. To the sheltered side
17. Remove intestines from fish
18. U.S. space agency
20. Wild Asian dog
22. Cringe
25. Scottish river
26. Church walkway
27. Offer
28. Ignited
31. Australian super-model
32. Bundle of money
33. Mexican currency
34. Prefix, new
35. Needlefish
36. Embers
37. Vandal
38. Angles

39. Shrink with fear
42. One's parents (Colloq)
43. Part of a circle
44. Molten rock
46. Fencing sword
50. Hazy
51. Test
52. Narrow opening
53. Freeze
54. Prefix, distant
55. Synchronize

DOWN
1. Two-up
2. Crude mineral
3. Flying mammal
4. Small spine
5. Conflict
6. Hawaiian dance
7. Before
8. Removed unwanted plants
9. Palm starch
10. 12th month of the Jewish calendar
11. Suffix, diminutive

19. Top card
21. Masculine pronoun
22. City in NW France
23. Anger
24. Capital of Norway
25. Carried out
27. Metal rod
28. Wife of Jacob
29. Small island
30. Throw
32. Ashen
33. Own
35. Esophagus
36. Spanish hero
37. Hello there
38. Burning gas
39. Muslim judge
40. Of urine
41. Pinnacle
42. Egg-shaped
45. Chop
47. 3 Thickness
48. An age
49. Etcetera

CROSSWORD Puzzle : 7

1	2	3	4		5	6	7	8		9	10	11
12					13					14		
15					16					17		
		18	19				20	21				
22	23	24				25						
26					27				28	29	30	
31				32			33					
34			35			36						
		37			38							
39	40	41			42							
43			44	45			46	47	48	49		
50			51				52					
53			54				55					

ACROSS
1. Ward off
5. Lunge
9. Ashen
12. Hip bones
13. Earthen pot
14. Before
15. Bites
16. Charge over property
17. Female ruff
18. Nimbus
20. Aver
22. Granular
25. Hive insect
26. Handkerchief
27. Sol
28. Large tree remnant
31. Against
32. Black
33. Persian fairy
34. - Maria, coffee liqueur
35. New Zealand parrot
36. Governor in Mogul India
37. Stomach
38. Corset

39. Jowl
42. Body of a ruined ship
43. U-turn (Colloq)
44. Adjoin
46. Sacred Egyptian bird
50. Normal
51. Swine
52. One of Columbus's ships
53. Mineral spring
54. Heed
55. Percussion instrument

DOWN
1. Fish part
2. Biblical high priest
3. Pinch
4. Colorful pullover garment
5. Foolishness
6. Potpourri
7. Island (France)
8. Norwegian arctic explorer
9. Once existed
10. Region
11. Never
19. Some

21. Plural of I
22. Steps descending to a river
23. Indian queen
24. Rectangular pier
25. However
27. Large body of water
28. Obscene
29. Spoken
30. Deride
32. Semite
33. Stationing car
35. Flightless parrot of New Zealand
36. Zero
37. Objective case of I
38. Courageous
39. Drinking vessels
40. Pile
41. Jaguarundi
42. Immense
45. Infant's protective garment
47. Prefix, life
48. Tavern
49. Droop

CROSSWORD Puzzle : 8

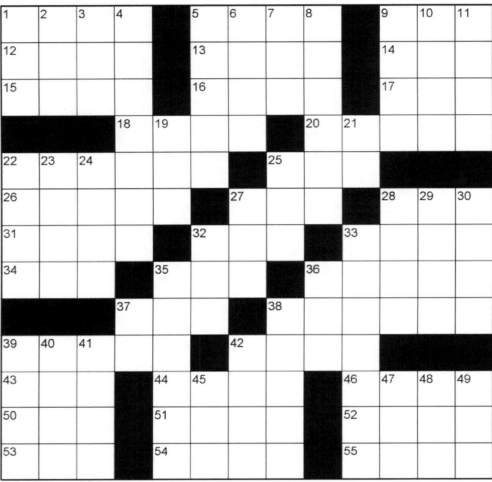

ACROSS
1. Monetary unit of Western Samoa
5. After deductions
9. The self
12. Matures
13. Island of Hawaii
14. Over there
15. Air duct opening
16. Frozen confections
17. Fabulous bird
18. Hasty
20. Abrade
22. Volcanic froth
25. New Guinea seaport
26. Digging tool
27. An age
28. An urban area
31. Foot part
32. Talk
33. Threesome
34. An explosive
35. Spoil
36. Pose
37. Musical instrument
38. Inflammatory elevation of the skin

39. Monetary unit of France
42. Bag
43. Atmosphere
44. Large trees
46. Christmas
50. Eccentric wheel
51. American state
52. Is indebted
53. Cathedral city
54. Bristle
55. Nurse

DOWN
1. 23rd letter of the Hebrew alphabet
2. Mature
3. Pet form of Leonard
4. Straddling
5. Sound
6. Every
7. Definite article
8. Pertaining to Tuscany
9. Jaguarundi
10. Stupid person
11. At one time
19. Top card

21. Masculine pronoun
22. Surreptitious, attention getting sound
23. On top of
24. Germinated grain
25. Throw lightly
27. Otic organ
28. Official language of Pakistan
29. Monetary unit of Cambodia
30. Tree trunk
32. Goad for driving cattle
33. Variety of tufted pigeon
35. Resembling mucus
36. Raincoat
37. Not off
38. Turkish governor
39. Visage
40. Monetary unit of Iran
41. Military body
42. Card game
45. Dined
47. Be indebted
48. Even (poet.)
49. Hallucinogenic drug

CROSSWORD Puzzle : 9

ACROSS
1. Motion picture
5. Spur
9. Gear wheel
12. Dutch cheese
13. Boss on a shield
14. Bullfight call
15. Republic in W Africa
16. Pleasing
17. Transfix
18. Camp shelter
20. Soft leather
22. Granular
25. - and outs, intricacies
26. Works for
27. Feline
28. Item of headwear
31. Eager
32. Edge
33. Drink to excess
34. Uncooked
35. Captained
36. Lift
37. Take to court
38. Tun

39. Chocolate substitute
42. Exclamations of surprise
43. America (Abbr)
44. Papal edict
46. Inwardly
50. Monetary unit of Japan
51. Personalities
52. Relax
53. Cushion
54. Ostrich-like bird
55. Clarets

DOWN
1. Prefix, whale
2. Revised form of Esperanto
3. Henpeck
4. Affecting emotion
5. Burlap
6. Exclude
7. Government broadcaster
8. Does not
9. Manage
10. Fetid
11. Hereditary factor
19. Abstract being

21. Objective case of we
22. Cog
23. Hindu music
24. In a line
25. Braggart (Colloq) (1.2)
27. Spanish hero
28. Coconut husk fibre
29. Church recess
30. Skin
32. Female ruff
33. Large-eyed, Indonesian monkey
35. Awkward sailor
36. Cheer
37. Therefore
38. Light wood
39. Pointed end
40. At sea
41. South African currency
42. Agave
45. Expression of disgust
47. Not
48. Hallucinogenic drug
49. Affirmative response

CROSSWORD Puzzle : 10

1	2	3	4		5	6	7	8		9	10	11
12					13					14		
15					16					17		
			18	19				20	21			
22	23	24				25						
26					27				28	29	30	
31				32				33				
34			35				36					
		37				38						
39	40	41			42							
43			44	45				46	47	48	49	
50			51				52					
53			54				55					

ACROSS
1. German Mrs
5. Mop
9. Leg
12. Nobleman
13. Muslim judge
14. Mount - , N.W. Qld. mining town
15. U.S. TV award
16. Bear constellation
17. Annihilate
18. Confidence trick
20. Breaks suddenly
22. Pickled
25. Prefix, the earth
26. Beginning
27. Young goat
28. Cyst envelope
31. Beats by tennis service
32. 9th letter of the Hebrew alphabet
33. Ear part
34. Prefix, foot
35. Clumsy person
36. Cubed
37. Once common, now banned, insecticide
38. Envoy
39. Got up
42. Capital of Switzerland
43. Battle
44. Australian super-model
46. Republic in SW Asia
50. Wood sorrel
51. Saturate
52. Weary
53. Fox
54. Pedal digits
55. Fencing sword

DOWN
1. A charge
2. Male sheep
3. Limb
4. Hero of the Odyssey
5. Military detachment
6. Fairly hot
7. Commercials
8. Tendentious
9. Suburb of Cairo
10. As soon as possible
11. Charts
19. Prefix, whale
21. Negative vote
22. Bath requisite
23. At one time
24. Second-hand
25. British, a fool
27. State of drowsy contentment
28. Caribbean dance music
29. Wrongfully assist
30. Yield
32. Make lace
33. Soft coal
35. Most peculiar
36. The (German)
37. Perform
38. Welsh vegetables
39. Study
40. Savoury Mexican dish
41. Toward the mouth
42. Blue-gray
45. Card game
47. Tear
48. Land measure
49. Born

CROSSWORD Puzzle : 11

ACROSS
1. 3 Sit for portrait
5. Great age
9. Legal right
12. Level
13. Floor covering
14. Avail of
15. Greek goddess of the earth
16. Crude minerals
17. Semite
18. Pout
20. Inter ashes
22. A piece of cotton
25. Yoko -
26. Shy from
27. Pig
28. Heavy weight
31. Greek god of war
32. Clumsy person
33. Mast
34. Colour
35. Young goat
36. Rumor
37. Indian dish
38. Planks
39. Esau's twin
42. First class (1-3)
43. Highest mountain in Crete
44. Unwrap
46. Faucets
50. Forefront
51. Young goats
52. Egg-shaped
53. Printer's measures
54. Current month
55. Depend

DOWN
1. Wooden pin
2. Eggs
3. Witness
4. Gives glazed finish to
5. Audibly
6. Ireland
7. Monad
8. Nuzzling
9. Fetish
10. Consumer
11. Stitched
19. Large tree
21. Negative vote
22. Type of automatic gear selector (1-3)
23. Fleet rodent
24. Regretted
25. Money (Slang)
27. Possessed
28. Travel
29. Fetid
30. Devices for fishing
32. Lubricant
33. Roman magistrate
35. Popular drama of Japan
36. French, good
37. Perform
38. Invigorate
39. Jitterbug
40. First man
41. Tins
42. Appends
45. A fool
47. Greeting
48. Mate
49. Wily

CROSSWORD Puzzle : 12

1	2	3	4		5	6	7	8		9	10	11
12					13					14		
15					16					17		
			18	19				20	21			
22	23	24					25					
26					27				28	29	30
31					32				33			
34				35				36				
			37				38					
39	40	41				42					
43				44	45				46	47	48	49
50				51					52		
53				54					55		

ACROSS
1. Seize
5. Stable attendant
9. That woman
12. Double curve
13. Skin
14. Indicate assent
15. Carry
16. Stringed instrument
17. Crude mineral
18. Timber tree
20. Havana resident
22. Conclusion
25. Sexless things
26. Fades
27. Long-leaved lettuce
28. Part of a circle
31. Finished
32. Grandmother
33. Off-Broadway theater award
34. - Kelly
35. Dog's foot
36. Beg
37. A month
38. Tipple
39. Ascend
42. Peaks
43. Assist
44. Elegance
46. Colours
50. Negative
51. Egyptian goddess of fertility
52. Capital of Norway
53. Before
54. Sprint
55. Long fish

DOWN
1. Torrid
2. The self
3. Seine
4. Baby who is teething
5. Wet slapping sound
6. Itch
7. Prefix, whale
8. Chooses
9. Scorning person
10. Israeli round dance
11. Paradise
19. Greek goddess of the dawn
21. Objective case of we
22. On top of
23. Surface a road
24. Toboggan
25. Charged particle
27. Crow call
28. In bed
29. Monetary unit of Iran
30. Yield
32. No
33. Comfortably familiar
35. Pale
36. Young dog
37. Objective case of I
38. Muscular tissue
39. Sensible
40. Jetty
41. Brink
42. Line of revolution
45. America (Abbr)
47. Avail of
48. Former measure of length
49. Distress signal

CROSSWORD Puzzle : 13

1	2	3	4		5	6	7	8		9	10	11
12					13					14		
15					16					17		
			18	19				20	21			
22	23	24					25					
26						27				28	29	30
31					32				33			
34				35				36				
			37				38					
39	40	41				42						
43				44	45				46	47	48	49
50				51					52			
53				54					55			

ACROSS
1. Vapour
5. Pierce with knife
9. Toothed fastener
12. Press clothes
13. U.S. State
14. Go wrong
15. Type of automatic gear selector (1-3)
16. Fur
17. An infusion
18. Shakespeare's river
20. Fawn
22. Torment
25. Decade
26. Concur
27. My, French (Plural)
28. Sharp projection
31. Shank
32. Young goat
33. Wise
34. Beldam
35. Gender
36. Fuming sulphuric acid
37. Large body of water

38. Anoints
39. The populous
42. On top of
43. Freeze
44. Peaks
46. Notes at scale's ends
50. An age
51. Compelled
52. Fencing sword
53. Large barrel
54. Personalities
55. Hire

DOWN
1. Spasm
2. An urban area
3. New Zealand bird
4. Maddens
5. Stupor
6. At that time
7. Sicken
8. Fencing thrusts
9. Greek letter
10. Angered
11. Make supplication

19. Victory sign
21. Not off
22. German composer
23. Taj Mahal site
24. Narcotic
25. Spread out for drying
27. Blend
28. Woman who killed Sisera
29. Fever
30. Jewels
32. New Zealand parrot
33. Thin
35. Til
36. Yoko -
37. Therefore
38. Church recesses
39. Food regimen
40. Colour of unbleached linen
41. Intend
42. Upswept hairdo
45. A delay
47. Open
48. Female bird
49. Become firm

CROSSWORD Puzzle : 14

1	2	3	4		5	6	7	8		9	10	11
12					13					14		
15					16					17		
			18	19				20	21			
22	23	24					25					
26						27				28	29	30
31					32				33			
34				35				36				
			37				38					
39	40	41				42						
43				44	45				46	47	48	49
50				51					52			
53				54					55			

ACROSS
1. Merit
5. Hairless
9. A failure
12. Prayer
13. Double curve
14. Finish
15. A particular
16. European mountain range
17. By way of
18. Jaguarundi
20. Oneness
22. Privateer
25. Revised form of Esperanto
26. Homer's epic
27. "The Raven" author
28. Corded fabric
31. Alter
32. Influenza
33. Trundle
34. Some
35. Wages
36. Torment
37. Assist
38. Subdebutante

39. Slow
42. Arm bone
43. Crude mineral
44. Harp-like instrument
46. Canter
50. - de Janeiro
51. Relax
52. Wallaroo
53. Even (poet.)
54. This thing
55. Something owing

DOWN
1. Prefix, over
2. High-pitched
3. Female ruff
4. Day of one's christening
5. French market town
6. Taj Mahal site
7. Meadow
8. Mislead
9. Hindu mother goddess
10. Military detachment
11. June 6, 1944
19. 10th letter of the Hebrew

alphabet
21. Negative vote
22. Hindu god of destruction
23. Dash
24. Well ventilated
25. Acknowledgement of debt
27. 3 Thickness
28. Thoroughfare
29. Otherwise
30. Plebeian
32. A craze
33. Discounted
35. Ice ax
36. Large barrel
37. Near to
38. Rain and snow
39. Tradition
40. A Great Lake
41. Lighting gas
42. Bear constellation
45. Exclamation of disgust
47. Regret
48. Sphere
49. Young child

CROSSWORD Puzzle : 15

1	2	3	4		5	6	7	8		9	10	11
12					13					14		
15					16					17		
			18	19				20	21			
22	23	24					25					
26						27				28	29	30
31				32					33			
34				35				36				
			37				38					
39	40	41				42						
43				44	45				46	47	48	49
50				51					52			
53				54					55			

ACROSS
1. Lively dances
5. Having wings
9. Long-sleeved linen vestment
12. European mountain range
13. Skeletal part
14. Not
15. Japanese wooden clog
16. Radar screen element
17. I have
18. Christmas
20. Book of maps
22. Noon
25. Prefix, life
26. Cow's milk sac
27. Seed vessel
28. Former coin of France
31. Scorch
32. Pig
33. Swimsuits
34. Utter
35. Beep horn
36. Patron Saint of beggars
37. Swindle
38. Roam

39. Ladle
42. Jumble
43. Attention-getting call
44. Eager
46. Wild revelry
50. Carp-like fish
51. Secure
52. Ostrich-like bird
53. Videlicet
54. Agitate
55. A fool

DOWN
1. Ewer
2. Anger
3. Gun (Slang)
4. Defame
5. Monastery of an abbot
6. Hang droopingly
7. Black bird
8. Settled debt
9. Indigo
10. Molten rock
11. Hive insects
19. Paddle

21. In the direction of
22. Rumple
23. Notion
24. June 6, 1944
25. Mire
27. Burst
28. Vended
29. Double curve
30. Former Soviet Union
32. Coxa
33. Small-time
35. Detour
36. Vapour
37. Depart
38. Person that wades
39. Switchblade
40. Basic monetary unit of Ghana
41. Town crier's call
42. High fidelity
45. Large tub
47. 17th letter of the Greek alphabet
48. Information
49. Synthetic yttrium aluminum
    garnet

CROSSWORD Puzzle : 16

ACROSS
1. Weary
5. Bushman's pack
9. New Zealand parrot
12. As soon as possible
13. Appendage
14. Doze
15. Flying mammals
16. Frizzy hair style
17. First woman
18. Is not
20. Promised
22. Looped
25. Female swan
26. Brother of Moses
27. Vapour
28. Hard-shelled fruit
31. At that time
32. Girl (Slang)
33. Hindu garment
34. Musical instrument
35. Bark sharply
36. Twilled cloth
37. Chatter
38. Football

39. Stolen
42. Bargain event
43. Israeli submachine gun
44. Jail
46. Daybreak
50. Grandmother
51. European mountain range
52. Fencing sword
53. Finish
54. Resembling ink
55. Something owing

DOWN
1. Label
2. Mount - , N.W. Qld. mining town
3. Rodent
4. Greek letter
5. Get up
6. Float through air
7. Atmosphere
8. Mittens
9. Understood
10. Roof overhang
11. Mimicked
19. Monetary unit of Japan

21. Not off
22. Roman censor
23. Island of Hawaii
24. Angered
25. Mate
27. Hiatus
28. Narcotics agent
29. Incite
30. Row
32. Sulky
33. Formally withdrew from
35. Yankee
36. The sun
37. Objective case of I
38. Woefully
39. Melody
40. Islamic call to prayer
41. Benevolent
42. Saturate
45. Vase
47. Primate
48. Spider's structure
49. Seine

CROSSWORD Puzzle : 17

ACROSS
1. Hindu teacher
5. Yield
9. Free
12. Islamic call to prayer
13. Upswept hairdo
14. Black bird
15. Beeps horn
16. Allows
17. Sexless things
18. Back of neck
20. Grecian architectural style
22. U.S. State
25. Writing fluid
26. Bowling sessions
27. Long-leaved lettuce
28. Indian dish
31. Vend
32. - and Yang
33. Mongolian desert
34. Finish
35. Small amount
36. Tout
37. Negative
38. Excrement

39. Spinnaker-like sail
42. Wan
43. - de Janeiro
44. Deride
46. Snake sound
50. Vase
51. Sea eagle
52. A Great Lake
53. Hive insect
54. Antlered beast
55. Hawaiian goose

DOWN
1. Talk
2. Israeli submachine gun
3. Knock with knuckles
4. Untangle
5. Guilt
6. Fencing sword
7. Once common, now banned, insecticide
8. Red dyes
9. Precipitation
10. Monetary unit of Peru
11. Circular plate

19. Commercials
21. Satisfactory
22. Proboscis
23. Level
24. Open country of S Africa
25. Charged particle
27. Spanish hero
28. Canines
29. Wrongfully assist
30. Italian currency
32. Synthetic yttrium aluminum garnet
33. Female black grouse
35. Joined
36. Expression of disgust
37. Negative vote
38. Gravel ridge
39. Larva
40. Ireland
41. Not any
42. Adolescent pimples
45. Crude mineral
47. Anger
48. Transgress
49. Witness

CROSSWORD Puzzle : 18

ACROSS
1. Saucy person
5. Difficult
9. Printer's measures
12. Tradition
13. Capital of Western Samoa
14. Female ruff
15. Monetary unit of China
16. English monk
17. Needlefish
18. Parched
20. Wild Asian dog
22. Battle
25. - kwon do (Korean martial art)
26. Fully developed
27. The sun
28. Jolt
31. Ore deposit
32. Dog variety
33. Wind instrument
34. Missus
35. New Guinea seaport
36. Tag
37. Firearm
38. Oxygenate

39. Chocolate substitute
42. Ireland
43. Biblical high priest
44. Inhabitant of a Baltic state
46. The villain in Othello
50. Sick
51. Gaelic
52. Ignore
53. Soap ingredient
54. Spool
55. Strikes

DOWN
1. 3 Thickness
2. Acknowledgement of debt
3. An age
4. Defendable
5. Custom
6. Mimicked
7. Free
8. Skillful
9. Therefore
10. Dinner or tea
11. Withered
19. Rodent

21. Masculine pronoun
22. Serene
23. Scent
24. Mires
25. To clothe
27. Take to court
28. Lively dance
29. Wrongfully assist
30. Death rattle
32. Kitchen utensil
33. Sully
35. Awkward sailor
36. Garland
37. Depart
38. Russian cooperative
39. Line roof
40. Friend
41. Anger
42. Otherwise
45. Land measure
47. Black bird
48. Remove intestines from fish
49. Observation

CROSSWORD Puzzle : 19

1	2	3	4		5	6	7	8		9	10	11
12					13					14		
15					16					17		
			18	19				20	21			
22	23	24					25					
26						27				28	29	30
31					32				33			
34				35				36				
			37				38					
39	40	41				42						
43				44	45				46	47	48	49
50				51					52			
53				54					55			

ACROSS
1. Ku Klux -
5. Girl
9. Play division
12. Wallaroo
13. Pain
14. Beetle
15. Matures
16. Ostrich-like bird
17. Highest mountain in Crete
18. Jealousy
20. Oriental peanut sauce
22. Republic in S central Africa
25. Charged particle
26. Situated on an axis
27. Kitchen utensil
28. Brassiere
31. Chinese dynasty
32. Total
33. Travel
34. Question
35. Make lace
36. Artist's medium
37. Grandmother
38. The game of hurling

39. New Mexico river
42. Undermines
43. Crude mineral
44. Drunkards
46. Monetary unit of Peru
50. Relation
51. Black
52. Merit
53. Superlative suffix
54. Rhythmic swing
55. Riding strap

DOWN
1. New Zealand parrot
2. Haul
3. Land measure
4. Fodder sack hung from horse's head
5. Immature insect
6. Having aches
7. That woman
8. Winter or spring
9. Entrance
10. Musical ending
11. Salver
19. Zero

21. Prefix meaning without
22. Ancient town in N Africa
23. Line of revolution
24. Type of fur
25. Braggart (Colloq) (1.2)
27. Place
28. Seethe
29. Mysterious symbol
30. Ostentatious
32. Japanese word of respect
33. Large-eyed, Indonesian monkey
35. Ornamental pendant consisting of a bunch of loose threads
36. Young dog
37. Negative vote
38. Contraction of has not
39. Jab
40. Greek goddess of strife
41. Monetary unit
42. Short take-off and landing aircraft
45. Japanese sash
47. Not
48. Prefix, three
49. Tavern

CROSSWORD Puzzle : 20

ACROSS
1. Verne's submariner
5. Spool
9. 17th letter of the Greek alphabet
12. Affirmative votes
13. Fencing sword
14. Jump
15. Long fish
16. Charged particles
17. Before
18. Ova
20. Son of Abraham
22. Estuarine lake
25. Card game
26. Around
27. A fool
28. Shoemaker's tool
31. Debutantes
32. Soap ingredient
33. Threesome
34. Biblical high priest
35. Top cricket hit
36. Seaport in NW Israel
37. Beep horn
38. Disencumbered
39. Ascend
42. Ooze
43. Feline
44. Questions
46. Exclude
50. Last month
51. Greek goddess of the earth
52. Wife of Jacob
53. Golf peg
54. Nervous
55. U.S. TV award

DOWN
1. Not
2. Optic organ
3. Actor, - Gibson
4. Bony
5. Rule
6. Epic poetry
7. Even (poet.)
8. A sore
9. Ostrich-like bird
10. Israeli round dance
11. Oil cartel
19. Obtained
21. Therefore
22. Burden
23. Cain's victim
24. Mongolian desert
25. Falsehood
27. Greek goddess of night
28. Parched
29. Spouse
30. A burden
32. Mouth part
33. Young frog
35. Green fodder preserved in store
36. Hasten
37. To exist
38. Iterate
39. Short tail
40. Wan
41. Suffix, diminutive
42. Surfboard fin
45. Morose
47. 13th letter of the Hebrew alphabet
48. Braggart (Colloq) (1.2)
49. Your

ABC PATH

ABC Path consists of a 5x5 grid. Around the edges of the grid are the letters B to Y. The letter A has been placed.

- The goal is to fill in all the cells so that all letters A to Y appear exactly once.

- Each letter must appear in the row, column, or diagonal corresponding to its clue.

- Each letter must be a neighbor to the letter that comes before and after it.

ABC PATH - 1

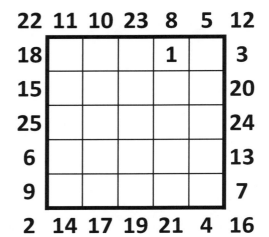

ABC PATH - 2

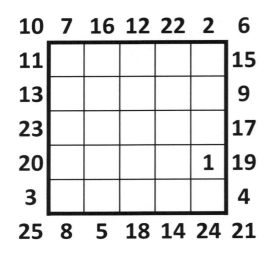

ABC PATH - 3

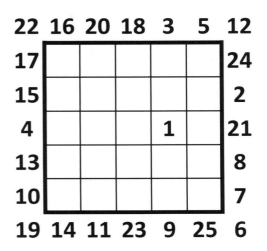

ABC PATH - 4

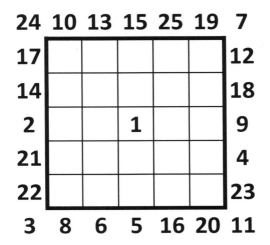

ABC PATH - 5

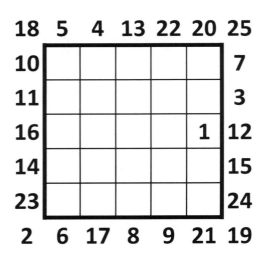

ABC PATH - 6

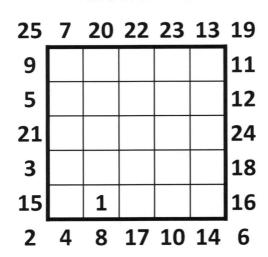

ABC PATH - 7

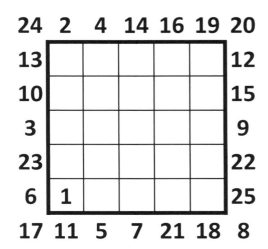

ABC PATH - 8

ABC PATH - 9

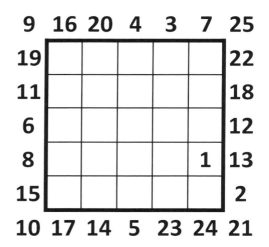

ABC PATH - 10

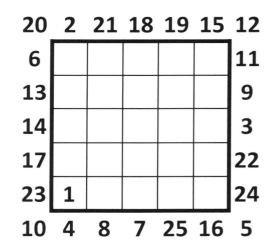

ABC PATH - 11

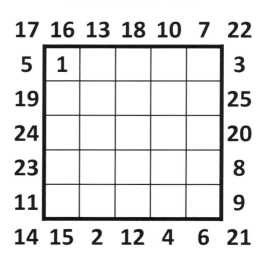

ABC PATH - 12

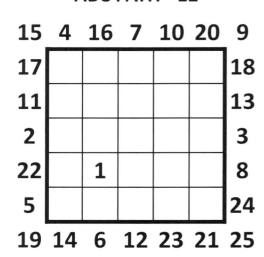

ABC PATH - 13

```
   10 17 13 20  8  3   6
18 ┌──┬──┬──┬──┬──┐
   │  │  │  │ 1│  │   2
22 ├──┼──┼──┼──┼──┤
   │  │  │  │  │  │  21
23 ├──┼──┼──┼──┼──┤
   │  │  │  │  │  │  16
 9 ├──┼──┼──┼──┼──┤
   │  │  │  │  │  │  25
14 ├──┼──┼──┼──┼──┤
   │  │  │  │  │  │  11
   └──┴──┴──┴──┴──┘
   24 15 19 12  5  4   7
```

ABC PATH - 14

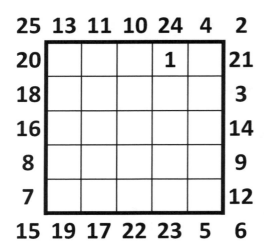

ABC PATH - 15

```
   25 10  7 15 16 18  17
14 ┌──┬──┬──┬──┬──┐
   │  │  │  │  │  │  13
23 ├──┼──┼──┼──┼──┤
   │  │  │  │  │  │  12
21 ├──┼──┼──┼──┼──┤
   │  │  │  │ 1│  │  11
20 ├──┼──┼──┼──┼──┤
   │  │  │  │  │  │   4
 5 ├──┼──┼──┼──┼──┤
   │  │  │  │  │  │   8
   └──┴──┴──┴──┴──┘
   24  9 22  6 19  2   3
```

ABC PATH - 16

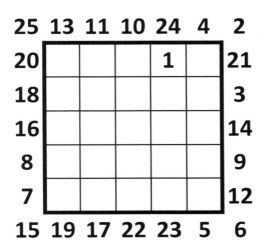

ABC PATH - 17

```
   22  4 21 25 18 14  12
 7 ┌──┬──┬──┬──┬──┐
   │  │  │  │  │  │   9
11 ├──┼──┼──┼──┼──┤
   │  │  │  │  │  │   6
24 ├──┼──┼──┼──┼──┤
   │  │  │  │  │  │   5
15 ├──┼──┼──┼──┼──┤
   │  │  │  │  │  │  19
17 ├──┼──┼──┼──┼──┤
   │  │  │ 1│  │  │   2
   └──┴──┴──┴──┴──┘
   20  3  8 23 10 13  16
```

ABC PATH - 18

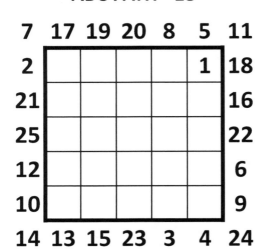

ABC PATH - 19

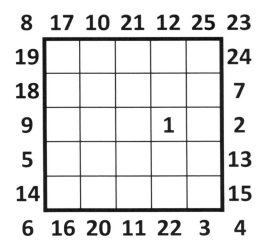

ABC PATH - 20

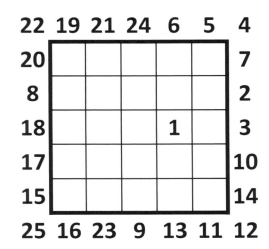

ABC PATH - 21

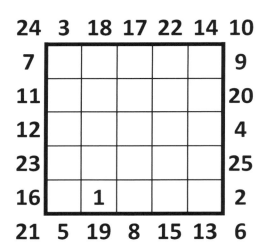

ABC PATH - 22

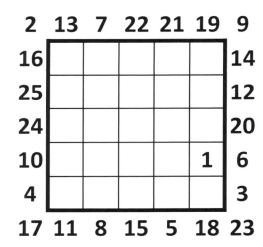

ABC PATH - 23

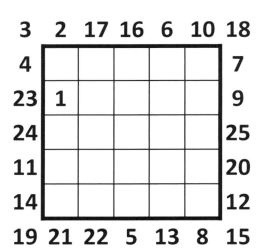

ABC PATH - 24

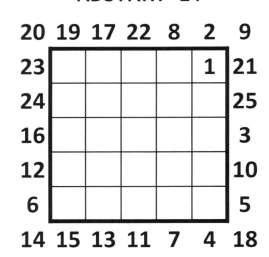

ABC PATH - 25

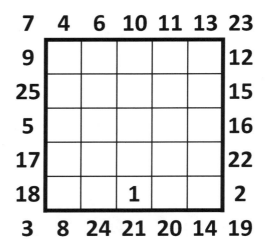

ABC PATH - 26

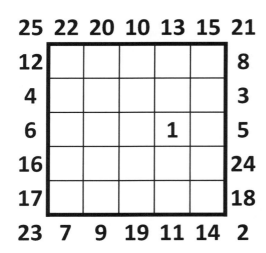

ABC PATH - 27

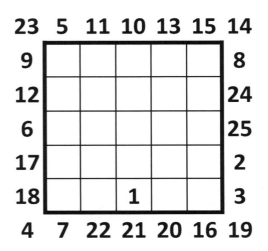

ABC PATH - 28

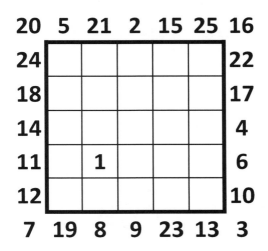

ABC PATH - 29

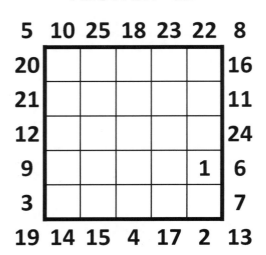

ABC PATH - 30

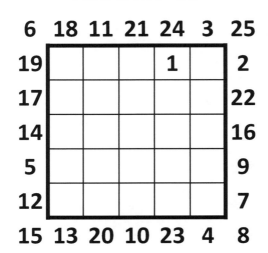

ABC PATH - 31

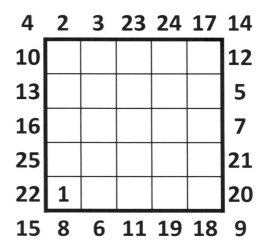

```
     4   2   3  23  24  17  14
   ┌───┬───┬───┬───┬───┐
10 │   │   │   │   │   │ 12
   ├───┼───┼───┼───┼───┤
13 │   │   │   │   │   │  5
   ├───┼───┼───┼───┼───┤
16 │   │   │   │   │   │  7
   ├───┼───┼───┼───┼───┤
25 │   │   │   │   │   │ 21
   ├───┼───┼───┼───┼───┤
22 │ 1 │   │   │   │   │ 20
   └───┴───┴───┴───┴───┘
    15   8   6  11  19  18   9
```

ABC PATH - 32

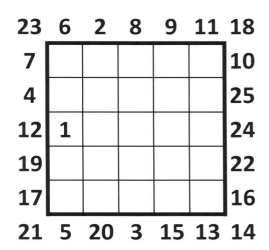

```
    23   6   2   8   9  11  18
   ┌───┬───┬───┬───┬───┐
 7 │   │   │   │   │   │ 10
   ├───┼───┼───┼───┼───┤
 4 │   │   │   │   │   │ 25
   ├───┼───┼───┼───┼───┤
12 │ 1 │   │   │   │   │ 24
   ├───┼───┼───┼───┼───┤
19 │   │   │   │   │   │ 22
   ├───┼───┼───┼───┼───┤
17 │   │   │   │   │   │ 16
   └───┴───┴───┴───┴───┘
    21   5  20   3  15  13  14
```

ABC PATH - 33

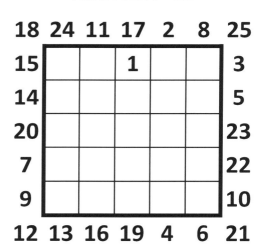

```
    18  24  11  17   2   8  25
   ┌───┬───┬───┬───┬───┐
15 │   │   │ 1 │   │   │  3
   ├───┼───┼───┼───┼───┤
14 │   │   │   │   │   │  5
   ├───┼───┼───┼───┼───┤
20 │   │   │   │   │   │ 23
   ├───┼───┼───┼───┼───┤
 7 │   │   │   │   │   │ 22
   ├───┼───┼───┼───┼───┤
 9 │   │   │   │   │   │ 10
   └───┴───┴───┴───┴───┘
    12  13  16  19   4   6  21
```

ABC PATH - 34

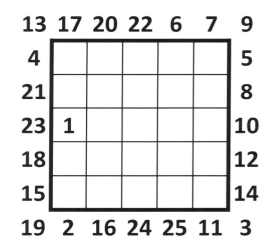

```
    13  17  20  22   6   7   9
   ┌───┬───┬───┬───┬───┐
 4 │   │   │   │   │   │  5
   ├───┼───┼───┼───┼───┤
21 │   │   │   │   │   │  8
   ├───┼───┼───┼───┼───┤
23 │ 1 │   │   │   │   │ 10
   ├───┼───┼───┼───┼───┤
18 │   │   │   │   │   │ 12
   ├───┼───┼───┼───┼───┤
15 │   │   │   │   │   │ 14
   └───┴───┴───┴───┴───┘
    19   2  16  24  25  11   3
```

ABC PATH - 35

```
    15  25   3   5  19  10  11
   ┌───┬───┬───┬───┬───┐
 2 │   │   │   │   │   │  8
   ├───┼───┼───┼───┼───┤
 6 │ 1 │   │   │   │   │  9
   ├───┼───┼───┼───┼───┤
12 │   │   │   │   │   │ 14
   ├───┼───┼───┼───┼───┤
16 │   │   │   │   │   │ 13
   ├───┼───┼───┼───┼───┤
21 │   │   │   │   │   │ 18
   └───┴───┴───┴───┴───┘
    22  23  24  20   7  17   4
```

ABC PATH - 36

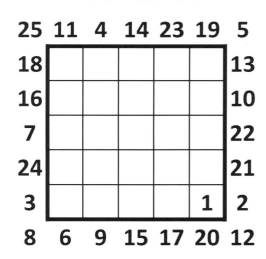

```
    25  11   4  14  23  19   5
   ┌───┬───┬───┬───┬───┐
18 │   │   │   │   │   │ 13
   ├───┼───┼───┼───┼───┤
16 │   │   │   │   │   │ 10
   ├───┼───┼───┼───┼───┤
 7 │   │   │   │   │   │ 22
   ├───┼───┼───┼───┼───┤
24 │   │   │   │   │   │ 21
   ├───┼───┼───┼───┼───┤
 3 │   │   │   │   │ 1 │  2
   └───┴───┴───┴───┴───┘
     8   6   9  15  17  20  12
```

ABC PATH - 37

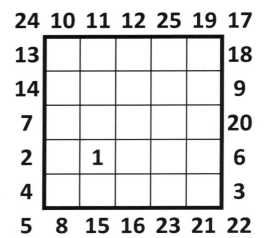

ABC PATH - 38

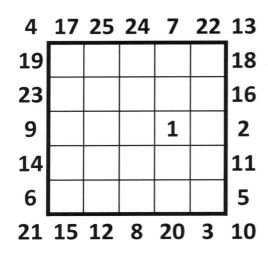

ABC PATH - 39

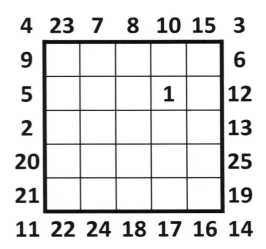

ABC PATH - 40

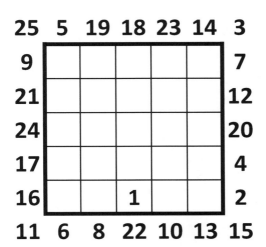

ABC PATH - 41

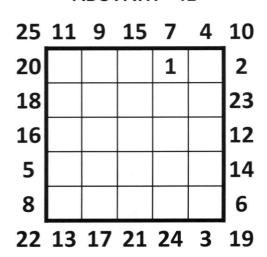

ABC PATH - 42

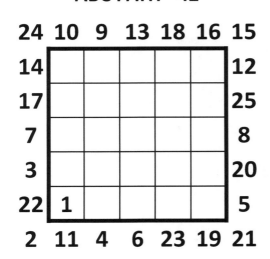

ABC PATH - 43

```
   12  9  5 20 25 15  6
14 [              ] 11
24 [              ] 16
18 [              ]  8
 7 [           1  ] 19
 2 [              ]  4
   22 10 23 13  3 17 21
```

ABC PATH - 44

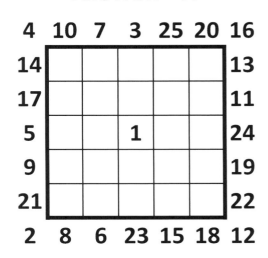

```
    4 10  7  3 25 20 16
14 [              ] 13
17 [              ] 11
 5 [      1       ] 24
 9 [              ] 19
21 [              ] 22
    2  8  6 23 15 18 12
```

ABC PATH - 45

```
   21 10 11  6 25 17 15
12 [              ] 14
16 [              ] 13
 5 [              ]  8
20 [              ]  2
23 [ 1            ] 22
    4  9  3 24 18 19  7
```

ABC PATH - 46

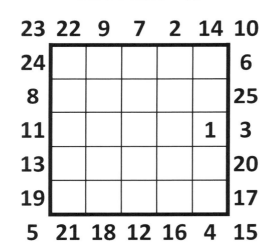

```
   23 22  9  7  2 14 10
24 [              ]  6
 8 [              ] 25
11 [           1  ]  3
13 [              ] 20
19 [              ] 17
    5 21 18 12 16  4 15
```

ABC PATH - 47

```
    2 22 20  4 14 11 21
 7 [              ]  8
10 [ 1            ]  6
13 [              ] 24
18 [              ] 19
17 [              ] 15
    9 23  3 25 16 12  5
```

ABC PATH - 48

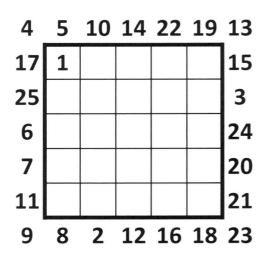

```
    4  5 10 14 22 19 13
17 [ 1            ] 15
25 [              ]  3
 6 [              ] 24
 7 [              ] 20
11 [              ] 21
    9  8  2 12 16 18 23
```

ABC PATH - 49

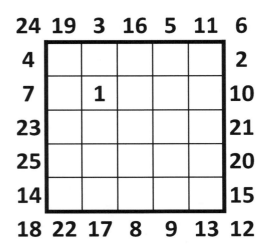

ABC PATH - 51

ABC PATH - 53

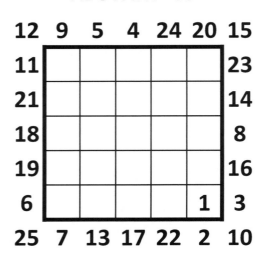

ABC PATH - 50

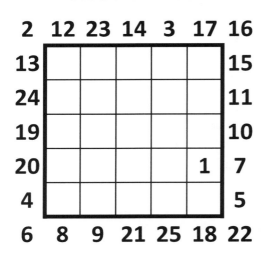

ABC PATH - 52

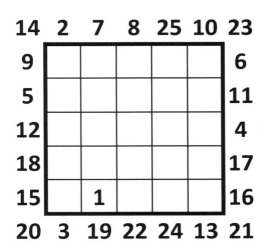

ABC PATH - 54

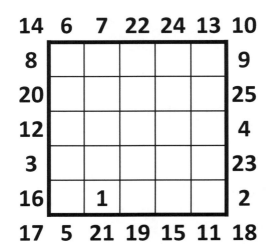

ABC PATH - 55

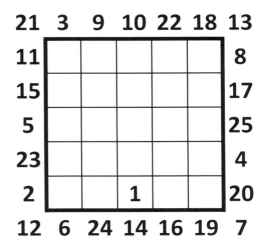

```
  21  3   9  10  22  18  13
11 ┌                      ┐ 8
15 │                      │ 17
 5 │                      │ 25
23 │                      │ 4
 2 │          1           │ 20
   └                      ┘
  12  6  24  14  16  19   7
```

ABC PATH - 56

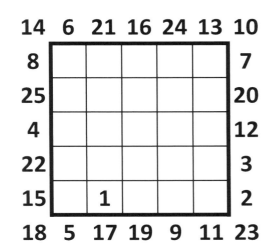

```
  14  6  21  16  24  13  10
 8 ┌                      ┐ 7
25 │                      │ 20
 4 │                      │ 12
22 │                      │ 3
15 │      1               │ 2
   └                      ┘
  18  5  17  19   9  11  23
```

ABC PATH - 57

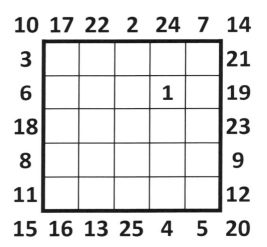

```
  10 17  22  2  24   7  14
 3 ┌                      ┐ 21
 6 │              1       │ 19
18 │                      │ 23
 8 │                      │ 9
11 │                      │ 12
   └                      ┘
  15 16  13  25   4   5  20
```

ABC PATH - 58

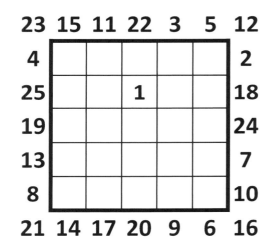

```
  23 15  11  22  3   5  12
 4 ┌                      ┐ 2
25 │          1           │ 18
19 │                      │ 24
13 │                      │ 7
 8 │                      │ 10
   └                      ┘
  21 14  17  20   9   6  16
```

ABC PATH - 59

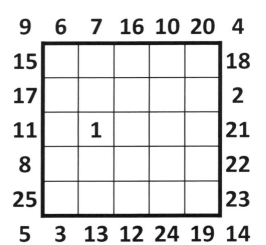

```
  9  6   7  16  10  20   4
15 ┌                      ┐ 18
17 │                      │ 2
11 │      1               │ 21
 8 │                      │ 22
25 │                      │ 23
   └                      ┘
   5  3  13  12  24  19  14
```

ABC PATH - 60

```
  21 14  17  18  9   7   8
10 ┌                      ┐ 11
12 │              1       │ 2
 3 │                      │ 15
16 │                      │ 20
23 │                      │ 22
   └                      ┘
  25 13  24   4   5   6  19
```

MAZES

The aim is to find your way to the exit after entering the maze. You can use your finger or a pen or pencil to trace your path
through the maze.

Intermediate

MAZE - 2

MAZE - 3

MAZE - 4

MAZE - 5

MAZE - 6

Intermediate

MAZE - 8

Intermediate

MAZE - 10

KRISS KROSS

Kriss kross is a great puzzle. Sometimes the grid starts empty and at other times there are words placed. Either way you must complete the grid.

Typically the puzzle will require some thinking ahead at certain stages; at other times there might be only one place where a word can go at a given time.

The words are usually sorted by length to make it easier for you to work out what can go where.

There is only one place a word can fit in the finished grid with a valid puzzle - in other words there is only one possible solution; each word is used and used exactly once.

In terms of tactics, the key method is always to see if there is a place that only one word can fit at a time. If not, then you will need to visualise the options in your head and say "if this word goes here, are there still valid placements for each word that this one will cross?" If no then you know that's not the right word; if yes then it could be, and repeat the logic with the next option and so on.

N° 1

mots de 4 lettres
Beth
Bibb
Boer
Moke
Ruse

mots de 5 lettres
Ceils
Louis
Sitar

mots de 6 lettres
Ambler
Straps

mot de 7 lettre
Delibes

mot de 8 lettre
Sea lions

mot de 9 lettre
Abduction

mots de 10 lettres
Codswallop
Earthquake
Impeccable
Middlebrow

mots de 12 lettres
Mournfulness
Standard lamp

mot de 14 lettre
Number cruncher

mot de 15 lettre
Proboscis monkey

N° 2

mots de 4 lettres
Rats
Scan
Silt
Surd
Tref
Turf

mots de 5 lettres
Dicey
Enure
Spiny
Unfix
Yeats

mots de 6 lettres
Coaxal
Elvish
Eureka
Static

mot de 8 lettre
Security

mot de 9 lettre
Dystopias

mot de 10 lettre
Superfoods

mot de 11 lettre
Sanatoriums

mot de 12 lettre
Underproduce

mots de 13 lettres
Conquistadors
Triglycerides

mot de 15 lettre
Entente cordiale

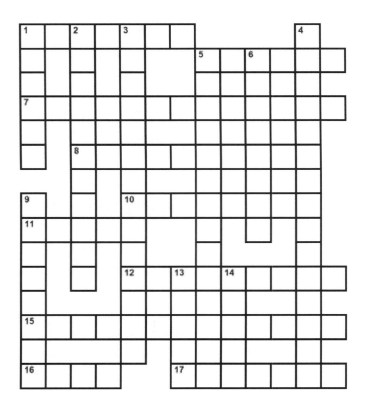

mots de 4 lettres
Chip
Lark

mots de 5 lettres
Diode
Tyson

mots de 6 lettres
Cravat
Oolite

mots de 7 lettres
Entraps
Puccini
Stand-in
Sunsuit
Taproom
Vellums

mot de 8 lettre
Davy lamp

mots de 9 lettres
Ruritania
Spritsail

mot de 11 lettre
Earthenware

mot de 12 lettre
Phoneticians

mot de 13 lettre
Weather strips

mot de 14 lettre
Relative clause

mot de 15 lettre
Personification

N° 4

mot de 4 lettre
Rusk

mots de 5 lettres
Ilium
Oxide
Usage

mots de 6 lettres
Avesta
Bomber

mots de 7 lettres
Antique
Mae West

mots de 8 lettres
Marsupia
Slimline
Took over

mot de 9 lettre
Triturate

mots de 10 lettres
Bafflement
Diesel fuel

mot de 11 lettre
Thalidomide

mots de 13 lettres
Splendiferous
Verbalisation

mot de 14 lettre
Quintessential

mot de 15 lettre
Sexual relations

mots de 4 lettres
Bows
Cree
Geek
Lads
Lens

mots de 5 lettres
Cowed
Eagle
Nepal
Shred
X-rays

mots de 6 lettres
Sauced
Xylose

mots de 8 lettres
Glassful
Ravagers

mots de 9 lettres
Guatemala
Other half
Portfolio

mots de 10 lettres
Hard-boiled
Last-minute
Manumitted

mot de 12 lettre
Extravaganza

mot de 15 lettre
Finishing school

mots de 4 lettres
G-man
Rums
Tags
Whig
Yarn

mots de 5 lettres
Roles
Worry

mot de 6 lettre
Tetany

mots de 7 lettres
Art deco
Glimmer

mots de 8 lettres
Eastings

Neonatal
Regrades

mot de 9 lettre
Roommates

mot de 10 lettre
Order paper

mots de 11 lettres
Admittances
Gerontology

mot de 12 lettre
Complainants

mot de 13 lettre
Trial-and-error

mot de 15 lettre
Plenipotentiary

N° 7

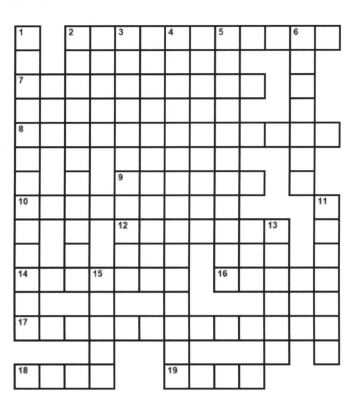

mots de 4 lettres
Faux
Tics

mots de 5 lettres
Affix
Eater
Gaged

mots de 6 lettres
Gagman
Usance

mots de 7 lettres
Cigaret
Eaten up
Nearing
Predate

mot de 10 lettre
End-stopped

mots de 11 lettres
Afterburner
Eye-catching
Unaddressed
Undeviating

mots de 13 lettres
Clear the decks
Reverberating
Staff sergeant

mot de 15 lettre
Duplex apartment

N° 8

mots de 4 lettres
Lido
Luxe
Rots
Vine
Wadi
Waif

mots de 5 lettres
Diana
Fagot
Lungi
Rasps
Villi

mot de 6 lettre
Gotten

mot de 7 lettre
Thereto

mots de 8 lettres
Hold over
Señorita
Therefor

mot de 9 lettre
Tractable

mots de 11 lettres
Stiff-necked
Well-behaved

mot de 12 lettre
Back and forth

mot de 13 lettre
Drinking songs

mot de 15 lettre
Hero-worshipping

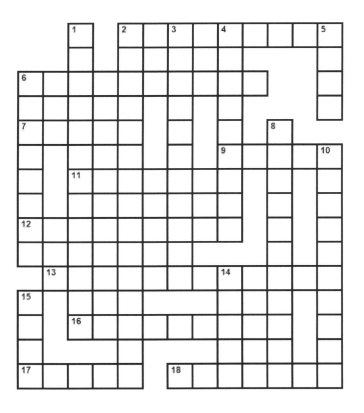

mots de 4 lettres
Bake
Damn
Pion
Yo-yo

mots de 5 lettres
Direr
Lupin
Taste
Velum

mots de 6 lettres
Gusher
Hailed
Volley

mots de 8 lettres
Basaltic
Roleplay
Seagrass

mots de 9 lettres
Intendeds
Neighbors
Submitted

mot de 10 lettre
Hypermedia

mot de 12 lettre
Armoured cars

mots de 13 lettres
Brainstorming
Ironing boards

mot de 15 lettre
Kind-heartedness

mots de 4 lettres
Gyro
Stew

mots de 5 lettres
Amahs
Cease
Often
Solfa

mots de 7 lettres
Osseous
Smegmas

mot de 8 lettre
Poseidon

mots de 9 lettres
Increases
Ownerless

Scimitars
Soi-disant

mots de 10 lettres
Paramedics
Subsystems

mots de 11 lettres
False bottom
Indian Ocean

mot de 12 lettre
Subconscious

mot de 13 lettre
Carillonneurs

mot de 15 lettre
Semi-abstraction

N° 11

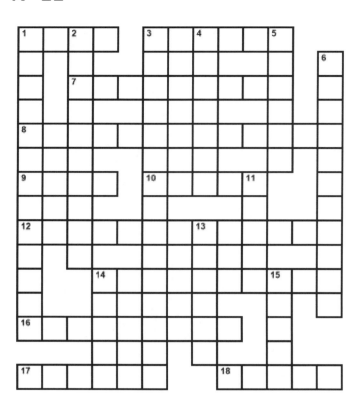

mots de 4 lettres	mots de 9 lettres
Pore	Paparazzo
Shim	Tricuspid

mots de 5 lettres	mots de 10 lettres
Delay	Impoverish
Essex	Profounder
Pecan	
Rayon	mot de 11 lettre
Xenon	Trespassers

mots de 6 lettres	mots de 13 lettres
Adders	Inventiveness
Shover	Resentfulness
Taunts	Self-important
Utopia	

mot de 7 lettre	mot de 15 lettre
Dwarves	Apartment houses

N° 12

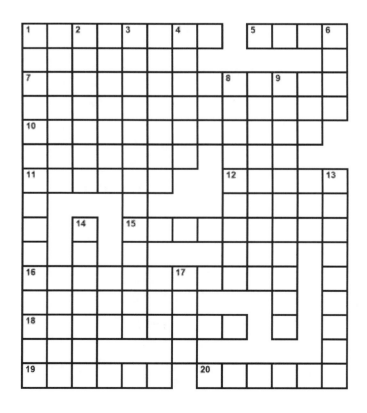

mots de 4 lettres	mots de 9 lettres
Bush	Enrapture
Cage	Errand boy
Hays	Ill humour
	Outweighs

mot de 5 lettre	mots de 11 lettres
Prude	Thumbscrews
	Tremulously

mots de 6 lettres	mot de 12 lettre
Elated	Greathearted
Midday	
Retest	mots de 13 lettres
Solace	Transparently
	Unsatisfiable

mots de 7 lettres	mot de 15 lettre
Abuttal	Categorizations
Nearest	

mot de 8 lettre
Censuses

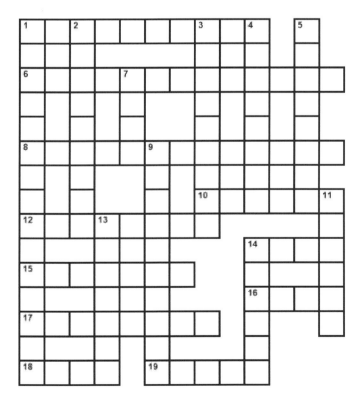

mots de 4 lettres
Ceca
Oral
Tong

mots de 5 lettres
Onion
Pitta
Salmi
Tests
Unmet

mots de 6 lettres
Emmets
Oppose
Wicket

mots de 9 lettres
Excitants
Steam pipe

mots de 10 lettres
Supplement
Triangulum

mot de 11 lettre
Gravimetric

mots de 12 lettres
Apostatising
Candid camera

mot de 13 lettre
Intelligences

mot de 14 lettre
Nonparticipant

mot de 15 lettre
Sensationalizes

---

mots de 4 lettres
Ghee
Lake
Rook
Toms

mot de 5 lettre
Glade

mots de 6 lettres
Loggie
NASDAQ
Q fever

mots de 7 lettres
Avowals
Immoral

mots de 8 lettres
Car parks

Gleaming
Lunacies
Sweetpea

mots de 9 lettres
Safe house
Titrating

mots de 10 lettres
Obligating
Systematic

mots de 13 lettres
Knockout drops
Reformatories

mot de 15 lettre
Shrinking violet

N° 15

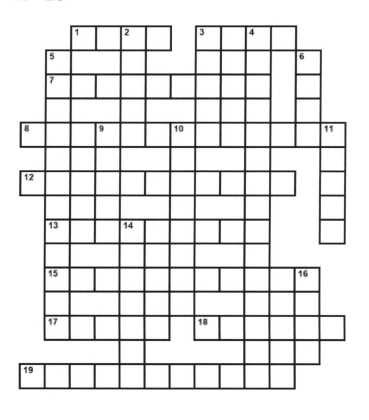

mots de 4 lettres
Coca
GATT
Hula
Rial

mots de 5 lettres
Copes
Inter
Local
Loire
Refit

mot de 6 lettre
Plenty

mot de 7 lettre
Zealand

mot de 8 lettre
Clear-cut

mots de 9 lettres
Net profit
Terza rima

mots de 11 lettres
Blind alleys
Catapulting
Photometric

mot de 12 lettre
Antithetical

mot de 13 lettre
Vivisectional

mot de 15 lettre
Authoritatively

N° 16

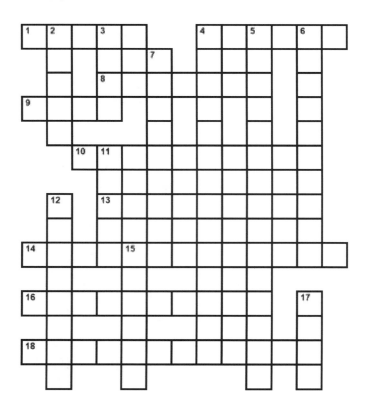

mots de 4 lettres
Doss
Hess
Wens

mots de 5 lettres
Ameer
Elite
Oaths

mots de 6 lettres
Canapé
Veiled

mot de 7 lettre
Sporran

mot de 8 lettre
Sleepers

mots de 9 lettres
Dominique
Inquorate

mots de 10 lettres
Meaningful
Portal vein
Specialist

mot de 12 lettre
Broken hearts

mot de 13 lettre
Redevelopment

mot de 14 lettre
Carbon monoxide

mot de 15 lettre
Noninflammatory

N° 17

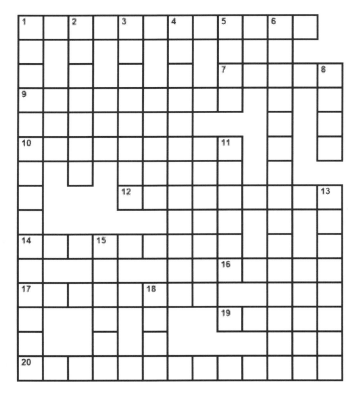

mots de 4 lettres
 Died
 Nobs
 Rube

mots de 5 lettres
 Mewls
 Miler
 Wrong

mot de 6 lettre
 Rights

mots de 7 lettres
 Mooting
 Thrombi

mot de 8 lettre
 Goofball

mots de 9 lettres
 Adeptness
 Deceiving
 Overdosed

mot de 10 lettre
 Engine room

mots de 11 lettres
 Assessments
 Overprinted
 Triceratops

mots de 13 lettres
 Bank statement
 Indiscretions
 United Kingdom

mot de 15 lettre
 Magnetic equator

N° 18

mots de 4 lettres
 Arvo
 Miso
 Rase

mots de 5 lettres
 Cargo
 Estop
 Scram

mots de 6 lettres
 Encase
 Vacate

mot de 7 lettre
 Bicarbs

mots de 8 lettres
 Ilmenite
 Soupçons

Truckage

mots de 9 lettres
 Embrittle
 Eparchies
 Flame tree
 Souvenirs

mots de 12 lettres
 Ingratiating
 Subsidiarity

mot de 13 lettre
 Numerologists

mots de 15 lettres
 Self-realisation
 Three-point turns

N° 19

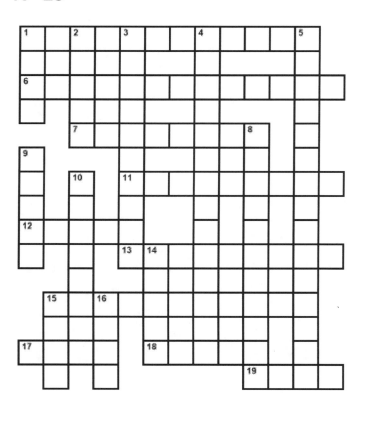

mots de 4 lettres
Aids
Clot
Kind
Quid
Seen

mots de 5 lettres
Knoll
Linac
Rider
Style
Yores

mot de 6 lettre
Honshu

mot de 8 lettre
Road rage

mots de 9 lettres

Syncretic
Thickhead

mot de 10 lettre
Onomastics

mots de 11 lettres
Ephemerides
Quadrillion

mot de 12 lettre
Corn on the cob

mot de 13 lettre
Old boy network

mot de 14 lettre
Hierarchically

mot de 15 lettre
Bermuda Triangle

N° 20

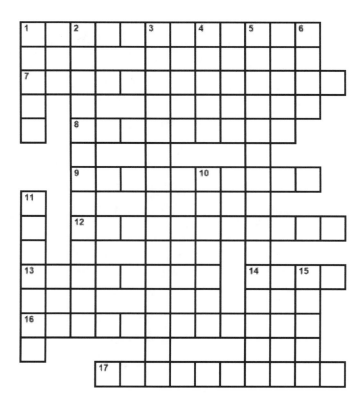

mots de 4 lettres
Lobs
Seep

mots de 5 lettres
Bantu
Fossa
Shack

mots de 7 lettres
Fattier
Poor law

mot de 8 lettre
Respighi

mot de 9 lettre
Astrakhan

mots de 10 lettres
Dysprosium
Nitrifying

mot de 11 lettre
Acceptances

mots de 12 lettres
Acrylic resin
Fecklessness

mots de 13 lettres
Curtain raiser
Sarcophaguses

mots de 15 lettres
Educationalists
Emperor penguins

SOLUTIONS

WORD SEARCH

```
. . L . . O . . . . . . .
. A D E S O R M I R P . .
C . E D O M E S T I C A T E
. R V G . P G H . . . . .
O R I G I N A L T . . . .
S L T . L N R . N . . . .
W C M . T M O . D . I . . M
. A E . . E Y P . R . C . A
. . N N L R R S S E N D A M R
B U T T E R C U P V R . . Y K
. N E O Y H T R A M M E L H
. E O C A N A U G R . . . O
G . . . . S G . . . . . R
. . . . D E B A U C H . .
. . . . D . . . . . . . .
```

```
. S . . . R . . . . . . . G
. . W T . E N A R R A T I O N
. Y . A V T . . . P B . . I
. . . L I R . R E L I A R T . V
D . R L B M . U C T . E . . I
U D . B O . . K C A B L L O R
M . . O G D U H . K . L . . H
P . . A I P . E C . E O Y . T
S B A R E L Y A T S E R O F R
T . . D . . J D . . R M . . U
E . . . I F L O A T A . . N
R . . H . P I H S . E . . D
. . . M O G U L . T . . L
. G E A R S H I F T S . E
F R E I G H T A G E . . .
```

```
. . D . . . M . . . . . .
. J I . . P . O . . . N .
. E D . A E B . O . . E .
. W N I B M A L . C P E
S E E B S . U . R K O E
O L L . P B L I W . R R
L E P . S I L V E R Y H H G
I R S . E A H T O C T . I
T . A . R Y D O A N L
A A . P C T . I O S A A I
I . S A I . U R O K S F
R U . S . M B E C R E I P
E L A T E M . . T M
. N . E U L A V . . A
. . . B . . . . . . C
```

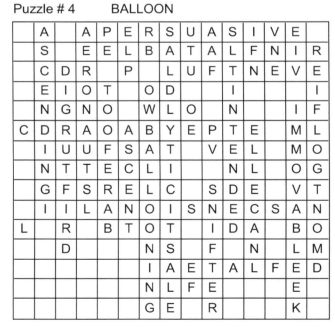

```
. A . A P E R S U A S I V E
. S . E E L B A T A L F N I R
. C D R . P . L U F T N E V E
. E I O T . O D . . I . . . I
. N G N O . W L O . N . I F
C D R A O A B Y E P T E . M L
I U U F S A T . V E L . M O
N T T E C L I . N L . O G
G F S R E L C . S D E . V T
I I L A N O I S N E C S A N
L R . B T O T . I D A . B O
. D . . N S . F . N . L M
. . . I A E T A L F E D
. . . N L F E . . . E
. . . G E R . . . K
```

Puzzle # 5 SCHOOL LUNCH IDEAS

	C	H	S	T	U	D	E	N	T			
	O	F	O	G	G	Y		K		A		
I		M	N			C	C			E	S	
N	E		T	P	S	A		E		N	T	D
N	R	M	O	D	E	R	N	I	T	Y		I
O	E			T	N	I	A	C		N	A	G
V	C	R		I	T	M	P	K		C	R	E
A	E	R	A		S	S	I	A		Y	O	S
T	P	R	A	E		B	R	O	R	U	S	T
I	T	B		G	B		O		O	N	Y	I
O	I			I		T	D	D		M		O
N	O	N	S	E	N	S	I	C	A	L	I	A	H	N
	N			U		D				K		
		J		U						I		
		T	S	A	L	C	O	N	O	C	I			A

Puzzle # 6 TOMATO

	I		W					S				
	N		O	E	N	C	O	U	R	A	G	E
	O		O	D	G		O					
	R		T	L	N	G		E	S	I	U	R	B
	A	P	O	E	L		E	C				B	R
I	C	L	R			I	E	A	H	E	A	T	E	D
T	A	A	P	P	L	E	T	N	D	S		T
T	M	N	E	E	R	G		A	I			A
E		T	D			H	L	M	V			R
H		O			S	A	O	Y	O			D
G				T	S	P	S	O		T		A
A			H	Y		A	H	P				T
P		G	H			S		I	I			I
S	L	I	P			T		C	N	C		O
T	N	A	R	G			A			X	Y	N

Puzzle # 7 TRAIN

			R						H	D	O	
U			E						S	R		
T				T	N	E	M	L	I	A	R	E	D
I				F	H	C	G	N	O			
L	O	O	K	O	U	T	A	I		I	B		C	T
I				R	N	L		F	Q	R	H	R
T			S	A	D	U		U	E	S	A
Y			I	T	C	L	N	P	A	S	S	I
E		C	E		T	E	G	P	D	D	I	E	N
	U	K	R	E	D	I	R	E	W	R	T	N	L
	D	J	U	D	O	R	A		A	C	R	O
		R			N	Y		M	T	A	E	A
	T	S	E	F	I	N	A	M	M	E	R	V	D
	C	A	V	A	L	C	A	D	E	P	O	
			O				M	L	G			

Puzzle # 8 FOUNDATION

	L		G									
	A	R	E	N	O	M	M	O	C			N
U	T	I	L	I	T	Y	Y		B		E	D
	N		D	C	N		E			T	R
L	E		N	C	O	R	S	E	L	E	T	A
E	M		U	M	F			Y		A	O
C	A	G	F	P	E		F	R		P	B
T	D	J	C	N	C	S	R	E	A		E
U	N	R	U	D	I	M	E	N	T	A	R	Y	S
R	U	O	L	D	S	D	C	T	B	D	A
E	F	C	V	A	L	N	R	I	I	A	B
S	K	E	I	B	I	U	O	L	L	M
H	E	N	R	Y	J	U	S	T	O	O
I	Y	T	B	M	T	R	S
P							G			

Puzzle # 9   ARMY TRAINING

	W	G	S	I	M	U	L	A	T	I	O	N		
D	P	A	N	Z	E	R	N	P	U	L	L	O	U	T
	A	C	N	I	B	A	S	I	C					
	R	U	O	G	D			H	A					R
D	T		Q	N	L	E		S		R			E	
	I			S	S	E	E	N			T	G	F	N
D	L	S			U	T	R			I	E	A	L	
R	L		C			H	L	E	B	M		C	R	L
A	E			I	E	S	O	T	E	R	I	C	T	E
U	R	V		R	P	V	C	N	A	L	E	U	L	B
G	Y		A		O	L		I	B	N			E	B
R		P		R			I	U	D		T		K	M
A	Y		P		L		P	N		E				U
E	D	U	C	A	T	E	D	A	E	H	M	U	R	D
R				R		T			D					

Puzzle # 10   GRADUATE

C	O	N	V	O	C	A	T	I	O	N				E
	N	O	I	T	A	R	B	I	L	A	C		L	G
		P			N	E	C	U	D	E	S	B		A
	N	H	I			A	X	E		E	A		F	L
	A		I	H			L	P	B	T			E	L
	M			G	S	I		I	E	A	E	M	H	O
	F			G	H	N	R	K	B	C	U	R	C	C
	F			W	R	T	R		M	U	T		O	T
	O		T			A	A	E	N	D	J		U	C
K	H	S			M		D	I	T	E	N	U	R	E
	R			O		I	T	U	L	N			S	P
E		E	L		C	N		R	A	N	I	M	E	S
	P	L	I	O					T					O
	I		N	C						E				R
D		E										D		P

Puzzle # 11   SHARK

			D	R	O	L	D	N	A	L			
			K	E	G	U	M	M	Y				
			R	M	M	A	K	O					
			A	M		O	P	A	N	G	A	T		R
		C	H	A	G	R	I	N		S		H		H
B	T		S	H	D	D	U	S	K	Y	T	R	C	I
E		H	U	O		A		E			E	U	N
N		R	N	A	I	H	C	A	L	E	S	R	C
C		S	U	A	L				P	L	H	I	O
H	A		S	F	S			O		E	O	D
L	S	H	I	R	K	H		T		H	R	S	O
E		S	B	O	N	N	E	T	H	E	A	D	I	N
Y	H	S	I	F	T	A	C	R		W		T
							K		Y

Puzzle # 12   ORIGINAL

				L	A	M	I	R	P	S			
	S	N		A			R	T		F			
	P	O	C		P	N	I	E		C	U	I	
	R	M		L	H	R	M	A	R	L	L	N	M
	I	Y		O	E	L		O		A	D	A
	N	T	T	W	R	V	D	N	T		V	A	G
R		G	E	N	U	I	N	E		S		E	M	I
E	Y	U	E	I	S	S	T	T	E		M	E	N
	T		U		M	C	P	C	R		I	N	A
		T	Q		A	O		E	I	R	T	T
		E		R	D			L	P	A	I
C	L	A	S	S	I	C	A	L	L	Y	F	L	V
		N		D	E	S	C	E	N	T	E	E
T	A	K	E	O	F	F						D
		C	U	N	P	L	O	U	G	H	E	D

Puzzle # 13 RELATIONSHIPS

G	R	A	M	M	A	R		M		S				C
	H					O	U							N
L		Y	I			W	O						O	Y
A		N		P		I	M	R				S		S
R	F	E			S	A		D	R		R			C
U	A	G		D	G	T		E		E	F	I	L	I
T	S	O	O	Y	Y	T	E	B	P	S	L	A	M	T
C	T	M	L			G	A	R		A	I	A		A
U	E	O		E			O	X	L	C	R		T	M
R	P	H			H	X		L	O	G		S		E
T	M				E	C	U	S	O	N			E	H
S	U		M	T	S	I	M	O	N	O	X	A	T	
	R		I		I	T	O	N			H	M		A
	T	C		O	N	N						T	Y	M
	S		N	A	M	A	T	C	H	M	A	K	E	R

Puzzle # 14 BABY SHOWER

L	L	L	A	B	D	D	O								
A		O		S											
R	T	S	N	E	T	S	I	R	H	C					
U	O	T			E			B	E						
D	D	O	E		S	R		D	A	N					
I	D	R		N		L		I			R	C	D		
P	L	K		T	U	C	S	L				R	E		
E	E			Y	I		C	H	I	C	K	E	N		
	R		L	R	C	O	A		Z		F	N			
		L	T		E		N	O	W	L	E	T			
	O	A						W		S					
H	P	M		U	N	B	O	R	N	O	G	A	W		
	M	S	P	A	R	K	L	E	R	U	E				
	A							H	N	R					
	M		S	C	I	R	T	E	T	S	B	O			

Puzzle # 15 PERSONAL FINANCE

	H			H			R						
N	O	I	G	I	L	E	R		D			I	D
S			D	R	V	U		I			N	E	
S	T	A	K	E			S			V	L	C	
E			N	S		C	L	T	I	P	O		
L		U	O	O	L		S	I	M			S	
E	E			U	O		I	C	M	E	D	I	U	M
C			N	R		B	N	E	P				I
A		T	K	C	L	I	N	T	E	R	E	S	T
F		N	T	E	R	T	I	A	R	Y	S		E
	A		F	P	A			G	S		I		G
B		F		R	E	K	I	N	O	M	V		D
	U		Y					N	O	E		U	
D	A	F	F	A	I	R	E	G	A	W	D		B
								L					

Puzzle # 16 SMARTPHONE

	Y	T	I	R	U	C	E	S	N	I			S	S
	R	F							N				P	W
	E		O					N	A	D	I	R	I	
	V	N	S	R		P			W	P		U	S	
I	I		U	A	G		E			A	P	C	H	
N	E			M	L	I		R		K	R	E	P	
C	C			E	V	V		T	A	E	B	R		
E	E			Y	R	A	A		M	L	I	C	K	
N	R			K		A	G	B		K				
S	C	R	E	E	N	O	T	L	E	L		O		
E	V	I	T	C	I	D	E	R	P	A	E	O		
D			D	E	K	C	O	L	B	C				
S	T	U	P	I	D		K	C	A	B	L	L	A	C
			T	E	L	E	P	H	O	N	E			

Puzzle # 17 — TRAIL RUNNING

				N	B				H	G		
N			T	N	A	T	I	M	O	C	N	O	C
F	A				C	I			L	L	I	G
U	I			K	S	L			U	T
S		D	A	P				G	I
E	O	P	E	R	A	T	I	O	N		R
U	D		A	M	C		W		R		W
Q	C	D	G		K	H	H		E	E	Y
I	O		Y	D	E	E	S	I		E	K	T
L	N		K	A	E	R	B	P	T	S		S	A
B	V		M	U	L	U	C	I	R	R	U	C	W
O	U		F	D	R	O	O	L	E	A		K
	L	F				R		V		V	L
	S	L				D	P	O	S	S	E
	E	F	O	O	T	I	N	G

Puzzle # 18 — MOBILE

	O	C	S	I	D	I	K	S	Y	N	C	
		F	K	A	E	R	B	L	I	A	J
	M	R	C	E	S			I	U		G		T
	T	O	L	U	E	N	E	N	C	R	E	N	H	Y
	D	A	O	N		L	E	T			N		A	L
		M		B		D	E	E			I	E	W	L
				L	L	N	T	R	A	I	L	E	R	O
			I	O	E			F	M		D			D
		G		C			A	A		N
		H			K		E	C		R	A
T						R		E			L
					T			T
				S			O
	S	T	R	E	A	M	I	N	G
							E

Puzzle # 19 — AIRCRAFT

		C						G			
			L				B		N		G	H
			D	E	H	S		I	I	Y	N	I
			I		A	T	T		R		I	G
		O	S		R	A	N	O	O	D	D	H
		R	E	K	Y	F	A	P	E	O		L	F
		I	M	R	P	F	L	N	S	M	C	O	L
	P	G	B	A	O	A		E	C		A	H	I
		O	A	B	N	U	I		E	E	N	M	E
	B	T	R	E	A		T	R		T	N		R
		U	K	D	C		H	B	S		O			A
	T	A	F	I		O			O	C	N
	W			F	L	S	T	E	W	A	R	D
			D	E	L				R	E
				T					D	W

Puzzle # 20 — EARTHQUAKE

E	C	N	A	B	R	U	T	S	I	D			A	
A			T	R	E	M	B	L	E	R	N	P	N
R				V	B	E	O			O	S
T	S	U	N	A	M	I	A	E	W	C	I	A	I	U
H	E	E	K	A	H	S	F	C	A	N	K	S	T	B
Q	G	R		P	T	A	A	L	T	L	C		P	D
U	A	T		A	L	S	Y	E	A	H	O		U	U
A	R	N	T	L	T	P	N	N	I		R		R	C
K	O	E		L	S	S	D	A		R	U	P	S	T
E	H	C	E	E	I				O				I	I
C	I		T	C	F		M				S	D	O
N	P	Y		P	H	E	N	O	M	E	N	O	N
A	E			R	A			I
			T			S	S
						M	M

WARSHIPS

WARSHIPS - 1 (Solution)   WARSHIPS - 2 (Solution)

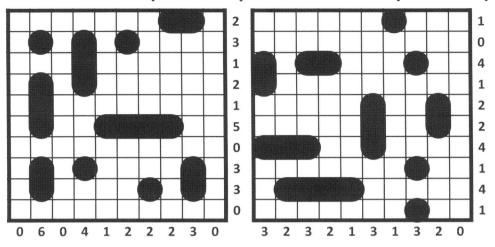

WARSHIPS - 3 (Solution)   WARSHIPS - 4 (Solution)

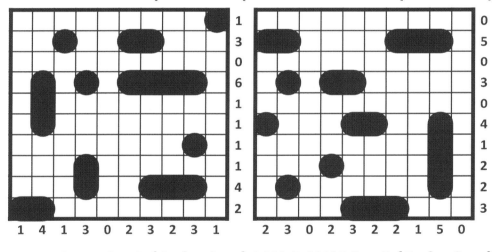

WARSHIPS - 5 (Solution)   WARSHIPS - 6 (Solution)

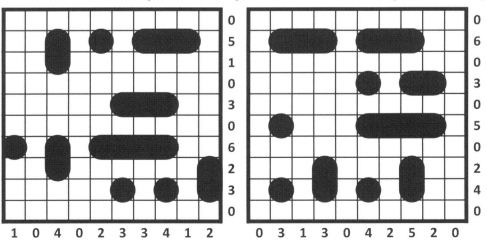

WARSHIPS - 7 (Solution)

Right: 2 2 0 2 0 5 3 3 3 0

Bottom: 0 3 1 4 0 5 1 2 2 2

WARSHIPS - 8 (Solution)

Right: 0 5 1 4 0 4 2 0 4 0

Bottom: 1 2 4 1 2 2 2 4 1 1

WARSHIPS - 9 (Solution)

Right: 0 1 4 2 0 5 4 3 0

Bottom: 3 0 5 1 2 1 4 1 2 1

WARSHIPS - 10

Right: 2 2 4 2 3 1 4 1 1 0

Bottom: 4 1 1 3 4 1 1 3 1 1

WARSHIPS - 11

Right: 2 3 0 6 1 1 5 0

Bottom: 1 3 1 4 1 2 2 3 3 0

WARSHIPS - 12

Right: 0 4 1 0 6 0 5 1 3 0

Bottom: 1 2 4 2 1 3 1 3 3 0

WARSHIPS - 13

WARSHIPS - 14

WARSHIPS - 15

WARSHIPS - 16

WARSHIPS - 17

WARSHIPS - 18

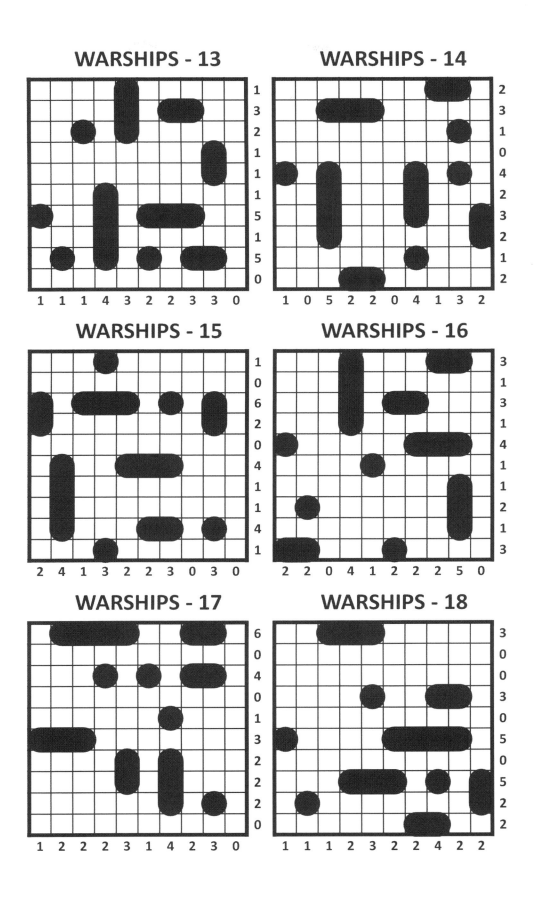

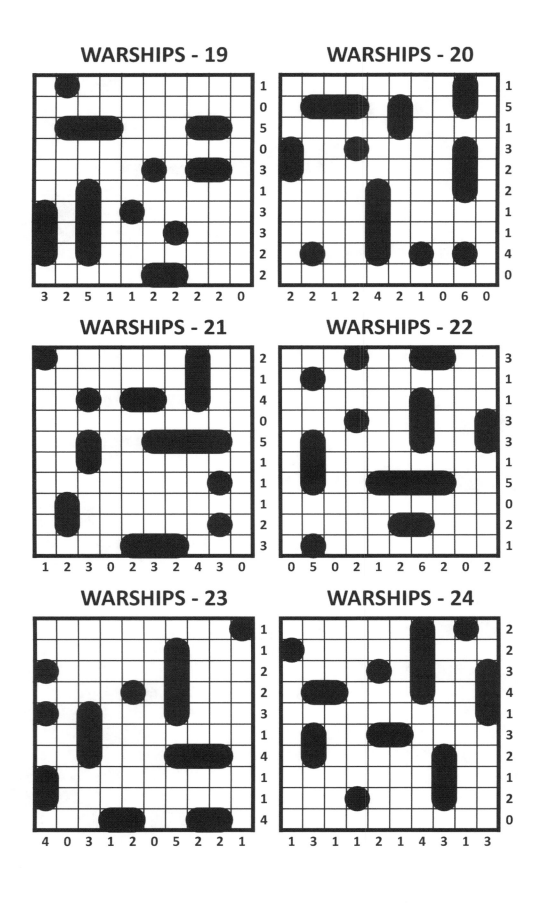

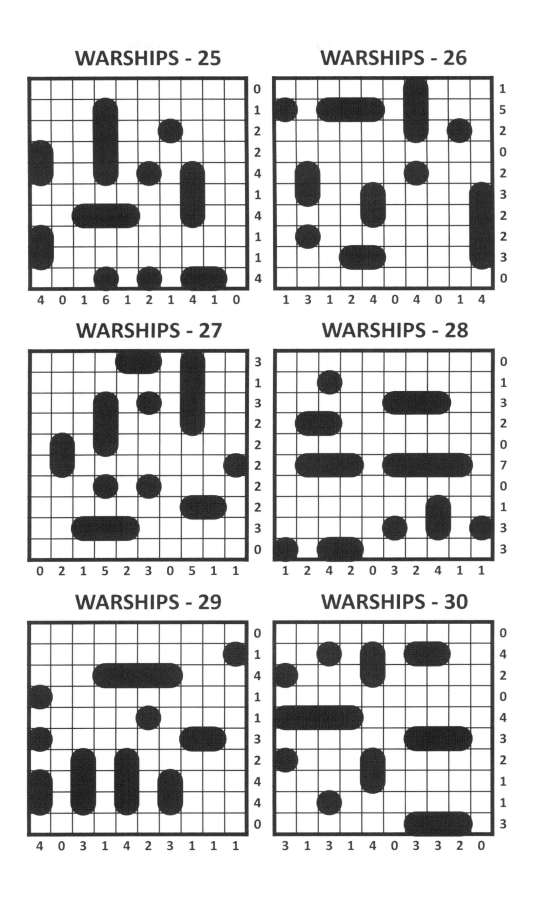

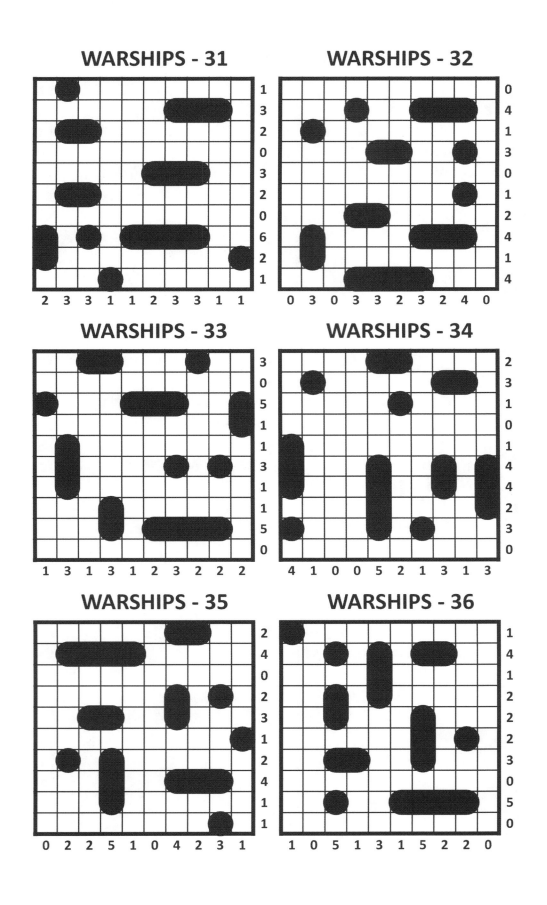

WARSHIPS - 37

WARSHIPS - 38

WARSHIPS - 39

WARSHIPS - 40

WARSHIPS - 41

WARSHIPS - 42

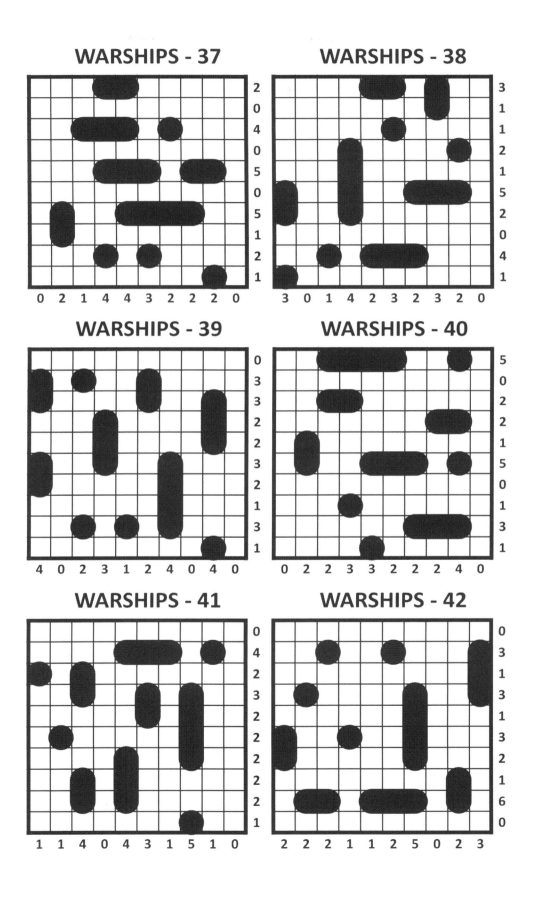

WARSHIPS - 43

WARSHIPS - 44

WARSHIPS - 45

WARSHIPS - 46

WARSHIPS - 47

WARSHIPS - 48

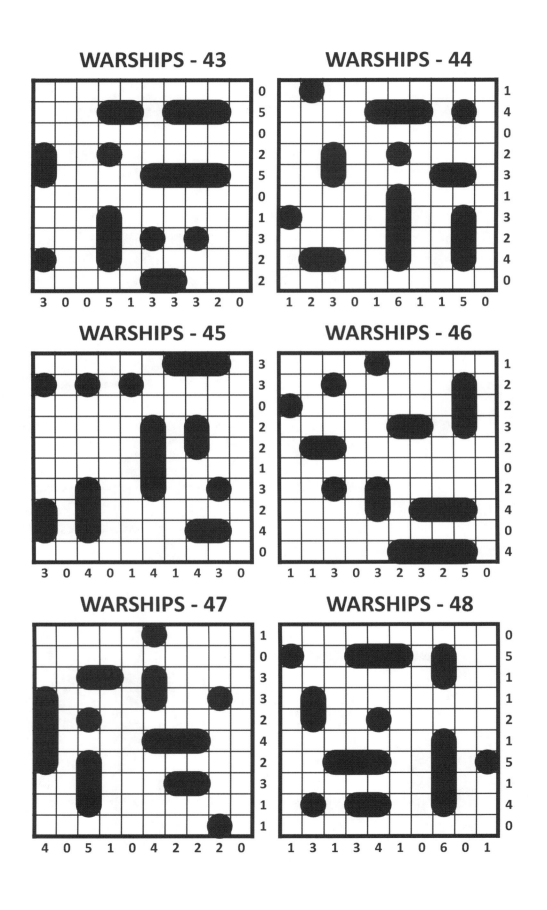

CALCULDOKU

GRID - 1 (Solution)

6	5	2	1	4	3
3	6	4	5	1	2
1	3	5	4	2	6
4	2	1	6	3	5
2	4	6	3	5	1
5	1	3	2	6	4

GRID - 2 (Solution)

6	1	4	3	5	2
2	4	3	5	6	1
5	3	2	6	1	4
1	5	6	4	2	3
3	6	1	2	4	5
4	2	5	1	3	6

GRID - 7 (Solution)

2	1	4	5	3	6
4	3	6	1	2	5
1	5	3	2	6	4
6	2	1	4	5	3
5	6	2	3	4	1
3	4	5	6	1	2

GRID - 8 (Solution)

5	4	6	2	1	3
2	6	4	3	5	1
6	2	3	1	4	5
4	3	1	5	2	6
3	1	5	4	6	2
1	5	2	6	3	4

GRID - 3 (Solution)

5	1	2	6	4	3
4	3	6	1	5	2
6	2	5	3	1	4
1	4	3	5	2	6
2	6	1	4	3	5
3	5	4	2	6	1

GRID - 4 (Solution)

6	1	5	3	4	2
4	6	2	5	3	1
1	3	6	4	2	5
3	5	4	2	1	6
2	4	1	6	5	3
5	2	3	1	6	4

GRID - 9 (Solution)

4	6	3	5	1	2
5	2	1	3	4	6
2	4	5	6	3	1
3	1	4	2	6	5
1	5	6	4	2	3
6	3	2	1	5	4

GRID - 10 (Solution)

1	6	3	4	2	5
4	1	2	6	5	3
2	5	6	3	4	1
5	3	4	2	1	6
3	2	5	1	6	4
6	4	1	5	3	2

GRID - 5 (Solution)

3	1	2	6	5	4
6	5	3	4	1	2
5	4	6	1	2	3
4	3	5	2	6	1
1	2	4	5	3	6
2	6	1	3	4	5

GRID - 6 (Solution)

6	4	2	5	3	1
5	2	4	1	6	3
2	5	3	6	1	4
1	3	5	2	4	6
3	1	6	4	5	2
4	6	1	3	2	5

GRID - 11 (Solution)

3	5	2	6	1	4
6	2	3	5	4	1
1	6	5	4	2	3
4	3	1	2	6	5
5	4	6	1	3	2
2	1	4	3	5	6

GRID - 12 (Solution)

6	4	5	1	3	2
4	2	3	5	1	6
3	6	1	4	2	5
2	3	4	6	5	1
1	5	6	2	4	3
5	1	2	3	6	4

GRID - 13 (Solution)

3	5	2	4	6	1
5	3	4	2	1	6
2	4	1	6	5	3
6	1	5	3	4	2
4	6	3	1	2	5
1	2	6	5	3	4

GRID - 14 (Solution)

2	6	4	5	3	1
3	2	6	4	1	5
1	3	5	6	2	4
6	5	1	2	4	3
4	1	2	3	5	6
5	4	3	1	6	2

GRID - 19 (Solution)

4	3	5	2	6	1
1	6	3	5	2	4
5	2	4	3	1	6
2	4	1	6	3	5
3	1	6	4	5	2
6	5	2	1	4	3

GRID - 20 (Solution)

6	5	2	4	3	1
5	6	1	3	4	2
1	2	4	5	6	3
4	3	6	2	1	5
2	4	3	1	5	6
3	1	5	6	2	4

GRID - 15 (Solution)

3	5	1	4	6	2
6	2	4	3	5	1
4	6	2	5	1	3
5	1	3	6	2	4
1	3	6	2	4	5
2	4	5	1	3	6

GRID - 16 (Solution)

6	5	2	1	3	4
2	6	4	5	1	3
5	3	6	2	4	1
1	4	5	3	2	6
3	2	1	4	6	5
4	1	3	6	5	2

GRID - 21 (Solution)

6	3	5	2	4	1
4	5	2	6	1	3
5	6	3	1	2	4
1	4	6	5	3	2
3	2	1	4	5	6
2	1	4	3	6	5

GRID - 22 (Solution)

6	5	4	3	2	1
5	3	1	2	6	4
2	4	6	1	3	5
1	2	3	5	4	6
4	1	2	6	5	3
3	6	5	4	1	2

GRID - 17 (Solution)

2	6	5	3	4	1
6	1	4	5	3	2
4	5	2	1	6	3
3	4	1	2	5	6
5	2	3	6	1	4
1	3	6	4	2	5

GRID - 18 (Solution)

6	1	2	4	3	5
5	4	6	1	2	3
2	3	5	6	1	4
4	5	1	3	6	2
3	6	4	2	5	1
1	2	3	5	4	6

GRID - 23 (Solution)

1	6	3	4	2	5
6	3	5	2	1	4
5	4	6	1	3	2
3	1	2	5	4	6
4	2	1	6	5	3
2	5	4	3	6	1

GRID - 24 (Solution)

1	4	6	2	5	3
3	6	4	5	1	2
6	1	3	4	2	5
2	3	5	6	4	1
4	5	2	1	3	6
5	2	1	3	6	4

GRID - 25 (Solution)

6	2	3	1	5	4
3	1	4	6	2	5
1	4	5	3	6	2
2	5	6	4	1	3
4	6	2	5	3	1
5	3	1	2	4	6

GRID - 26 (Solution)

4	5	1	3	6	2
6	2	3	5	4	1
5	6	2	4	1	3
3	1	4	6	2	5
2	3	6	1	5	4
1	4	5	2	3	6

GRID - 31 (Solution)

5	2	1	3	6	4
6	4	3	1	5	2
4	6	5	2	1	3
3	1	2	5	4	6
1	3	6	4	2	5
2	5	4	6	3	1

GRID - 32 (Solution)

5	1	3	6	2	4
2	6	1	3	4	5
1	2	4	5	3	6
6	4	5	2	1	3
4	3	6	1	5	2
3	5	2	4	6	1

GRID - 27 (Solution)

6	1	4	2	3	5
5	3	2	1	4	6
1	2	6	3	5	4
2	4	1	5	6	3
3	6	5	4	1	2
4	5	3	6	2	1

GRID - 28 (Solution)

5	6	3	4	1	2
3	4	5	1	2	6
4	2	1	6	3	5
6	1	2	5	4	3
1	3	6	2	5	4
2	5	4	3	6	1

GRID - 33 (Solution)

4	5	6	2	1	3
6	3	5	1	4	2
5	4	2	3	6	1
1	6	3	4	2	5
2	1	4	5	3	6
3	2	1	6	5	4

GRID - 34 (Solution)

5	2	4	3	6	1
2	3	1	4	5	6
1	6	5	2	3	4
3	1	6	5	4	2
6	4	3	1	2	5
4	5	2	6	1	3

GRID - 29 (Solution)

1	3	5	4	6	2
5	1	4	6	2	3
3	6	2	5	4	1
2	5	6	3	1	4
4	2	3	1	5	6
6	4	1	2	3	5

GRID - 30 (Solution)

6	3	5	2	4	1
1	2	4	5	6	3
4	5	1	6	3	2
2	4	3	1	5	6
5	6	2	3	1	4
3	1	6	4	2	5

GRID - 35 (Solution)

6	4	1	5	2	3
1	5	6	2	3	4
4	2	5	3	6	1
3	1	2	6	4	5
5	6	3	4	1	2
2	3	4	1	5	6

GRID - 36 (Solution)

6	2	5	4	1	3
5	4	6	2	3	1
4	6	1	3	5	2
2	1	3	6	4	5
1	3	2	5	6	4
3	5	4	1	2	6

GRID - 37 (Solution)

2	6	5	3	1	4
5	3	4	1	6	2
6	4	3	5	2	1
1	2	6	4	5	3
3	1	2	6	4	5
4	5	1	2	3	6

GRID - 38 (Solution)

4	5	6	3	1	2
6	1	2	5	3	4
5	2	3	1	4	6
1	3	4	6	2	5
2	6	1	4	5	3
3	4	5	2	6	1

GRID - 43 (Solution)

1	6	5	3	4	2
2	4	1	5	6	3
6	1	3	2	5	4
4	2	6	1	3	5
5	3	2	4	1	6
3	5	4	6	2	1

GRID - 44 (Solution)

5	1	4	3	2	6
1	4	3	5	6	2
6	2	5	1	4	3
4	3	6	2	5	1
3	5	2	6	1	4
2	6	1	4	3	5

GRID - 39 (Solution)

3	6	1	5	2	4
5	3	2	4	6	1
6	4	5	2	1	3
1	5	6	3	4	2
2	1	4	6	3	5
4	2	3	1	5	6

GRID - 40 (Solution)

2	4	1	6	5	3
4	2	6	5	3	1
5	6	4	3	1	2
3	1	5	4	2	6
6	3	2	1	4	5
1	5	3	2	6	4

GRID - 45 (Solution)

6	3	2	1	4	5
3	4	5	2	6	1
2	5	1	4	3	6
1	6	4	3	5	2
5	1	3	6	2	4
4	2	6	5	1	3

GRID - 46 (Solution)

2	6	3	1	4	5
1	3	4	2	5	6
3	2	5	4	6	1
4	5	2	6	1	3
5	1	6	3	2	4
6	4	1	5	3	2

GRID - 41 (Solution)

3	5	1	6	2	4
5	4	2	1	3	6
1	3	6	2	4	5
2	1	5	4	6	3
4	6	3	5	1	2
6	2	4	3	5	1

GRID - 42 (Solution)

6	5	3	1	4	2
1	2	5	4	3	6
3	6	2	5	1	4
2	4	1	6	5	3
4	1	6	3	2	5
5	3	4	2	6	1

GRID - 47 (Solution)

3	2	6	1	4	5
2	3	5	4	6	1
1	6	3	2	5	4
5	4	2	3	1	6
4	5	1	6	2	3
6	1	4	5	3	2

GRID - 48 (Solution)

6	4	1	5	2	3
5	3	6	4	1	2
1	5	2	3	6	4
3	6	5	2	4	1
2	1	4	6	3	5
4	2	3	1	5	6

GRID - 49 (Solution)

2	6	4	1	5	3
3	4	2	5	6	1
6	3	5	4	1	2
4	2	1	6	3	5
5	1	3	2	4	6
1	5	6	3	2	4

GRID - 50 (Solution)

1	4	2	3	6	5
3	6	5	4	1	2
4	3	6	2	5	1
6	1	3	5	2	4
2	5	1	6	4	3
5	2	4	1	3	6

GRID - 55 (Solution)

6	3	4	1	2	5
4	5	6	2	1	3
2	1	5	6	3	4
5	4	2	3	6	1
3	2	1	4	5	6
1	6	3	5	4	2

GRID - 56 (Solution)

4	2	6	5	3	1
2	5	3	6	1	4
1	4	5	3	6	2
5	6	2	1	4	3
6	3	1	4	2	5
3	1	4	2	5	6

GRID - 51 (Solution)

1	6	5	4	2	3
6	2	3	5	1	4
3	1	4	6	5	2
4	5	2	3	6	1
2	4	6	1	3	5
5	3	1	2	4	6

GRID - 52 (Solution)

6	5	3	2	4	1
2	4	6	5	1	3
1	2	5	3	6	4
4	3	1	6	2	5
5	1	2	4	3	6
3	6	4	1	5	2

GRID - 57 (Solution)

4	3	2	1	5	6
3	5	1	4	6	2
1	4	6	2	3	5
6	2	5	3	1	4
5	1	4	6	2	3
2	6	3	5	4	1

GRID - 58 (Solution)

4	6	1	5	3	2
5	1	4	3	2	6
6	5	3	2	1	4
2	3	6	1	4	5
1	2	5	4	6	3
3	4	2	6	5	1

GRID - 53 (Solution)

3	6	5	4	2	1
6	4	1	5	3	2
4	2	3	1	6	5
2	1	6	3	5	4
5	3	4	2	1	6
1	5	2	6	4	3

GRID - 54 (Solution)

3	5	4	1	2	6
5	4	3	2	6	1
2	1	5	6	3	4
6	3	1	4	5	2
1	6	2	5	4	3
4	2	6	3	1	5

GRID - 59 (Solution)

6	5	2	4	3	1
1	3	4	6	2	5
5	1	6	2	4	3
3	2	5	1	6	4
2	4	1	3	5	6
4	6	3	5	1	2

GRID - 60 (Solution)

1	6	3	4	5	2
5	3	4	2	6	1
3	4	2	5	1	6
4	5	1	6	2	3
6	2	5	1	3	4
2	1	6	3	4	5

SUDOKU

SUDOKU - 1 (Solution)
```
6 1 8 | 3 9 2 | 4 5 7
9 5 7 | 1 6 4 | 8 3 2
2 3 4 | 7 8 5 | 9 1 6
5 2 6 | 9 1 3 | 7 8 4
4 8 3 | 5 7 6 | 1 2 9
7 9 1 | 4 2 8 | 5 6 3
1 4 5 | 2 3 7 | 6 9 8
3 6 9 | 8 4 1 | 2 7 5
8 7 2 | 6 5 9 | 3 4 1
```

SUDOKU - 2 (Solution)
```
1 2 4 | 7 9 5 | 6 3 8
3 7 9 | 8 1 6 | 5 4 2
6 8 5 | 3 4 2 | 7 1 9
7 6 8 | 1 5 3 | 2 9 4
5 9 2 | 4 8 7 | 1 6 3
4 1 3 | 6 2 9 | 8 5 7
9 5 6 | 2 3 8 | 4 7 1
2 4 7 | 9 6 1 | 3 8 5
8 3 1 | 5 7 4 | 9 2 6
```

SUDOKU - 7 (Solution)
```
1 5 9 | 2 3 6 | 4 8 7
4 3 2 | 1 8 7 | 9 6 5
7 8 6 | 5 9 4 | 3 2 1
5 4 8 | 7 1 9 | 2 3 6
2 6 7 | 4 5 3 | 8 1 9
3 9 1 | 6 2 8 | 7 5 4
8 7 4 | 3 6 5 | 1 9 2
9 2 5 | 8 7 1 | 6 4 3
6 1 3 | 9 4 2 | 5 7 8
```

SUDOKU - 8 (Solution)
```
8 6 2 | 1 4 9 | 3 5 7
4 3 9 | 7 2 5 | 1 6 8
7 5 1 | 6 3 8 | 4 9 2
3 2 5 | 9 1 4 | 7 8 6
1 7 4 | 8 6 2 | 5 3 9
6 9 8 | 3 5 7 | 2 1 4
2 4 6 | 5 8 1 | 9 7 3
5 8 7 | 2 9 3 | 6 4 1
9 1 3 | 4 7 6 | 8 2 5
```

SUDOKU - 3 (Solution)
```
2 3 9 | 8 5 1 | 7 4 6
6 5 7 | 3 4 2 | 9 1 8
4 1 8 | 6 9 7 | 3 2 5
7 6 1 | 5 3 9 | 4 8 2
8 2 5 | 1 7 4 | 6 3 9
9 4 3 | 2 8 6 | 1 5 7
5 7 2 | 9 1 3 | 8 6 4
3 9 6 | 4 2 8 | 5 7 1
1 8 4 | 7 6 5 | 2 9 3
```

SUDOKU - 4 (Solution)
```
5 7 2 | 1 6 3 | 8 9 4
6 1 4 | 8 2 9 | 5 3 7
9 3 8 | 5 4 7 | 6 2 1
4 2 1 | 3 5 8 | 9 7 6
7 5 3 | 6 9 2 | 4 1 8
8 6 9 | 4 7 1 | 3 5 2
3 4 6 | 7 1 5 | 2 8 9
2 8 7 | 9 3 6 | 1 4 5
1 9 5 | 2 8 4 | 7 6 3
```

SUDOKU - 9 (Solution)
```
8 4 7 | 3 5 2 | 6 1 9
6 2 3 | 9 1 8 | 5 7 4
5 9 1 | 6 4 7 | 8 2 3
4 5 2 | 1 8 3 | 7 9 6
7 6 9 | 5 2 4 | 1 3 8
3 1 8 | 7 6 9 | 2 4 5
9 8 5 | 4 7 1 | 3 6 2
2 7 4 | 8 3 6 | 9 5 1
1 3 6 | 2 9 5 | 4 8 7
```

SUDOKU - 10 (Solution)
```
2 1 5 | 8 6 4 | 9 3 7
8 7 9 | 5 1 3 | 6 4 2
4 3 6 | 2 7 9 | 8 5 1
7 9 1 | 6 3 8 | 4 2 5
6 8 4 | 7 2 5 | 3 1 9
3 5 2 | 9 4 1 | 7 6 8
9 2 8 | 3 5 6 | 1 7 4
1 6 7 | 4 8 2 | 5 9 3
5 4 3 | 1 9 7 | 2 8 6
```

SUDOKU - 5 (Solution)
```
8 5 1 | 3 4 9 | 7 6 2
6 3 7 | 8 1 2 | 5 9 4
9 4 2 | 6 5 7 | 1 8 3
1 6 4 | 2 3 8 | 9 5 7
2 7 5 | 9 6 1 | 3 4 8
3 8 9 | 4 7 5 | 2 1 6
7 9 8 | 5 2 6 | 4 3 1
5 1 3 | 7 8 4 | 6 2 9
4 2 6 | 1 9 3 | 8 7 5
```

SUDOKU - 6 (Solution)
```
3 6 1 | 5 9 4 | 8 2 7
8 5 4 | 2 1 7 | 3 6 9
9 7 2 | 3 8 6 | 1 4 5
6 2 7 | 1 5 8 | 4 9 3
4 8 3 | 9 7 2 | 5 1 6
5 1 9 | 4 6 3 | 2 7 8
7 9 5 | 8 4 1 | 6 3 2
2 4 8 | 6 3 9 | 7 5 1
1 3 6 | 7 2 5 | 9 8 4
```

SUDOKU - 11 (Solution)
```
3 1 9 | 7 2 8 | 5 4 6
4 8 6 | 1 3 5 | 7 2 9
7 2 5 | 4 6 9 | 3 8 1
6 3 1 | 9 4 2 | 8 7 5
9 7 2 | 5 8 1 | 6 3 4
5 4 8 | 3 7 6 | 1 9 2
2 9 3 | 6 5 7 | 4 1 8
8 6 7 | 2 1 4 | 9 5 3
1 5 4 | 8 9 3 | 2 6 7
```

SUDOKU - 12 (Solution)
```
2 5 7 | 1 4 6 | 3 8 9
8 1 9 | 3 2 7 | 6 5 4
3 6 4 | 5 8 9 | 2 7 1
4 9 6 | 8 3 2 | 5 1 7
1 8 3 | 7 9 5 | 4 2 6
5 7 2 | 4 6 1 | 8 9 3
7 2 8 | 6 1 3 | 9 4 5
6 4 5 | 9 7 8 | 1 3 2
9 3 1 | 2 5 4 | 7 6 8
```

82

SUDOKU - 13 (Solution)
```
5 1 7 | 3 4 2 | 9 8 6
4 3 8 | 1 9 6 | 2 7 5
9 6 2 | 7 8 5 | 4 1 3
6 7 1 | 2 3 8 | 5 4 9
8 2 4 | 5 7 9 | 3 6 1
3 5 9 | 4 6 1 | 8 2 7
1 4 6 | 8 5 3 | 7 9 2
7 9 3 | 6 2 4 | 1 5 8
2 8 5 | 9 1 7 | 6 3 4
```

SUDOKU - 14 (Solution)
```
8 3 9 | 2 5 7 | 4 1 6
1 5 4 | 6 8 3 | 9 2 7
6 7 2 | 9 4 1 | 5 3 8
5 9 7 | 4 6 2 | 3 8 1
3 6 1 | 8 7 9 | 2 5 4
4 2 8 | 3 1 5 | 7 6 9
9 8 6 | 5 3 4 | 1 7 2
2 1 3 | 7 9 8 | 6 4 5
7 4 5 | 1 2 6 | 8 9 3
```

SUDOKU - 19 (Solution)
```
6 3 9 | 1 4 5 | 2 8 7
2 7 1 | 9 3 8 | 4 6 5
4 8 5 | 7 2 6 | 1 9 3
5 9 4 | 2 7 3 | 6 1 8
3 2 8 | 6 5 1 | 9 7 4
1 6 7 | 8 9 4 | 5 3 2
8 4 6 | 5 1 7 | 3 2 9
9 1 3 | 4 8 2 | 7 5 6
7 5 2 | 3 6 9 | 8 4 1
```

SUDOKU - 20 (Solution)
```
8 2 6 | 9 1 4 | 7 5 3
4 7 9 | 8 5 3 | 6 2 1
5 3 1 | 7 2 6 | 9 8 4
1 8 2 | 4 7 5 | 3 9 6
6 4 7 | 3 9 8 | 5 1 2
3 9 5 | 1 6 2 | 8 4 7
9 1 8 | 2 3 7 | 4 6 5
2 6 3 | 5 4 9 | 1 7 8
7 5 4 | 6 8 1 | 2 3 9
```

SUDOKU - 15 (Solution)
```
2 8 5 | 1 3 4 | 9 7 6
9 3 1 | 5 7 6 | 2 4 8
7 6 4 | 2 8 9 | 5 3 1
8 4 7 | 9 1 3 | 6 5 2
3 9 2 | 7 6 5 | 1 8 4
5 1 6 | 8 4 2 | 7 9 3
1 2 8 | 4 9 7 | 3 6 5
4 7 3 | 6 5 1 | 8 2 9
6 5 9 | 3 2 8 | 4 1 7
```

SUDOKU - 16 (Solution)
```
5 4 1 | 7 2 8 | 3 9 6
3 9 6 | 5 1 4 | 2 7 8
2 8 7 | 3 6 9 | 1 4 5
4 6 2 | 1 9 7 | 5 8 3
8 1 9 | 4 5 3 | 6 2 7
7 5 3 | 6 8 2 | 4 1 9
1 3 4 | 9 7 5 | 8 6 2
9 2 5 | 8 4 6 | 7 3 1
6 7 8 | 2 3 1 | 9 5 4
```

SUDOKU - 21 (Solution)
```
2 1 7 | 6 5 9 | 8 4 3
3 6 8 | 1 7 4 | 2 5 9
9 4 5 | 2 8 3 | 1 6 7
6 2 4 | 3 1 7 | 9 8 5
7 8 1 | 5 9 2 | 6 3 4
5 3 9 | 8 4 6 | 7 2 1
4 9 2 | 7 3 8 | 5 1 6
8 5 3 | 9 6 1 | 4 7 2
1 7 6 | 4 2 5 | 3 9 8
```

SUDOKU - 22 (Solution)
```
7 1 6 | 5 9 3 | 4 8 2
4 8 2 | 1 7 6 | 9 3 5
3 5 9 | 2 4 8 | 7 1 6
2 9 5 | 8 1 4 | 3 6 7
6 7 8 | 3 5 9 | 1 2 4
1 3 4 | 6 2 7 | 5 9 8
5 2 7 | 9 6 1 | 8 4 3
9 4 3 | 7 8 2 | 6 5 1
8 6 1 | 4 3 5 | 2 7 9
```

SUDOKU - 17 (Solution)
```
5 8 1 | 3 9 7 | 6 2 4
7 9 2 | 1 6 4 | 5 8 3
6 4 3 | 8 2 5 | 9 1 7
3 5 6 | 4 1 2 | 7 9 8
9 7 8 | 5 3 6 | 1 4 2
2 1 4 | 9 7 8 | 3 5 6
1 3 7 | 2 4 9 | 8 6 5
4 6 5 | 7 8 1 | 2 3 9
8 2 9 | 6 5 3 | 4 7 1
```

SUDOKU - 18 (Solution)
```
8 3 4 | 1 2 7 | 6 5 9
9 6 2 | 4 5 3 | 7 8 1
5 7 1 | 9 8 6 | 4 2 3
2 4 6 | 3 1 8 | 9 7 5
7 5 9 | 6 4 2 | 3 1 8
1 8 3 | 5 7 9 | 2 6 4
3 9 8 | 2 6 1 | 5 4 7
6 1 5 | 7 9 4 | 8 3 2
4 2 7 | 8 3 5 | 1 9 6
```

SUDOKU - 23 (Solution)
```
3 6 7 | 9 4 8 | 5 1 2
9 4 5 | 6 2 1 | 3 7 8
8 1 2 | 5 3 7 | 6 9 4
2 8 1 | 4 7 3 | 9 6 5
6 7 9 | 8 1 5 | 4 2 3
5 3 4 | 2 6 9 | 7 8 1
7 5 3 | 1 8 6 | 2 4 9
4 9 8 | 7 5 2 | 1 3 6
1 2 6 | 3 9 4 | 8 5 7
```

SUDOKU - 24 (Solution)
```
1 2 7 | 3 9 4 | 8 6 5
5 3 9 | 7 8 6 | 1 4 2
8 6 4 | 2 5 1 | 3 7 9
3 8 5 | 9 7 2 | 6 1 4
2 7 6 | 4 1 5 | 9 3 8
9 4 1 | 6 3 8 | 5 2 7
4 9 3 | 8 6 7 | 2 5 1
6 1 2 | 5 4 9 | 7 8 3
7 5 8 | 1 2 3 | 4 9 6
```

83

84

85

SUDOKU - 25 (Solution)

7	2	6	1	9	8	5	4	3
8	1	4	6	5	3	2	9	7
5	3	9	2	7	4	8	1	6
1	6	8	5	4	7	3	2	9
9	5	3	8	2	1	7	6	4
4	7	2	9	3	6	1	8	5
3	8	5	4	6	2	9	7	1
6	9	1	7	8	5	4	3	2
2	4	7	3	1	9	6	5	8

SUDOKU - 26 (Solution)

6	8	1	9	4	2	3	7	5
7	2	5	3	8	6	9	1	4
4	3	9	7	5	1	2	8	6
9	6	3	5	2	7	1	4	8
1	7	8	6	9	4	5	3	2
5	4	2	8	1	3	7	6	9
8	1	7	2	6	9	4	5	3
2	5	4	1	3	8	6	9	7
3	9	6	4	7	5	8	2	1

SUDOKU - 31 (Solution)

6	8	1	7	4	5	9	2	3
9	4	7	6	3	2	1	8	5
3	5	2	1	9	8	6	4	7
7	3	5	8	1	4	2	6	9
4	6	9	3	2	7	5	1	8
2	1	8	9	5	6	7	3	4
8	9	6	4	7	1	3	5	2
5	7	4	2	6	3	8	9	1
1	2	3	5	8	9	4	7	6

SUDOKU - 32 (Solution)

2	4	6	7	5	8	3	9	1
1	9	7	4	6	3	5	2	8
3	8	5	9	2	1	7	6	4
6	5	1	2	7	4	8	3	9
4	3	9	5	8	6	2	1	7
7	2	8	3	1	9	4	5	6
8	7	3	1	9	5	6	4	2
9	6	4	8	3	2	1	7	5
5	1	2	6	4	7	9	8	3

SUDOKU - 27 (Solution)

9	4	8	6	7	1	3	2	5
5	3	2	8	4	9	1	7	6
7	1	6	5	3	2	4	9	8
3	5	9	7	8	4	6	1	2
6	7	1	3	2	5	9	8	4
8	2	4	9	1	6	7	5	3
4	6	7	2	9	8	5	3	1
2	9	5	1	6	3	8	4	7
1	8	3	4	5	7	2	6	9

SUDOKU - 28 (Solution)

5	6	1	7	3	4	9	2	8
3	4	2	9	8	5	7	6	1
9	8	7	6	2	1	3	5	4
1	9	8	4	7	2	6	3	5
4	3	6	5	9	8	2	1	7
7	2	5	3	1	6	4	8	9
6	7	4	1	5	3	8	9	2
8	1	9	2	6	7	5	4	3
2	5	3	8	4	9	1	7	6

SUDOKU - 33 (Solution)

9	3	4	7	5	1	6	8	2
5	2	8	3	4	6	9	1	7
1	6	7	8	9	2	3	4	5
3	5	1	4	8	7	2	6	9
6	8	9	1	2	3	5	7	4
4	7	2	9	6	5	1	3	8
7	9	3	2	1	8	4	5	6
2	1	5	6	7	4	8	9	3
8	4	6	5	3	9	7	2	1

SUDOKU - 34 (Solution)

4	5	6	1	3	7	8	9	2
7	9	8	5	2	6	3	4	1
1	3	2	4	8	9	5	6	7
9	6	5	3	1	2	4	7	8
3	8	1	7	9	4	2	5	6
2	4	7	8	6	5	9	1	3
8	1	4	6	5	3	7	2	9
5	2	3	9	7	1	6	8	4
6	7	9	2	4	8	1	3	5

SUDOKU - 29 (Solution)

5	6	4	9	2	1	7	3	8
9	1	8	5	3	7	6	4	2
3	7	2	4	6	8	9	1	5
7	5	1	8	9	4	3	2	6
8	3	9	6	1	2	4	5	7
4	2	6	3	7	5	8	9	1
2	4	7	1	8	3	5	6	9
6	8	5	2	4	9	1	7	3
1	9	3	7	5	6	2	8	4

SUDOKU - 30 (Solution)

8	4	9	1	5	7	6	2	3
5	1	3	6	9	2	7	8	4
7	6	2	3	8	4	9	1	5
6	8	5	7	4	1	3	9	2
4	2	7	5	3	9	1	6	8
9	3	1	8	2	6	5	4	7
1	9	8	4	7	3	2	5	6
3	5	6	2	1	8	4	7	9
2	7	4	9	6	5	8	3	1

SUDOKU - 35 (Solution)

5	6	9	1	7	3	4	8	2
3	7	4	5	2	8	9	6	1
2	8	1	4	6	9	7	3	5
9	4	6	8	5	7	2	1	3
1	5	2	6	3	4	8	7	9
7	3	8	2	9	1	5	4	6
4	9	3	7	1	2	6	5	8
6	2	7	3	8	5	1	9	4
8	1	5	9	4	6	3	2	7

SUDOKU - 36 (Solution)

7	2	5	3	6	4	8	9	1
4	8	9	5	1	7	3	2	6
3	6	1	8	9	2	7	4	5
5	1	4	9	3	6	2	7	8
8	9	6	2	7	5	1	3	4
2	7	3	4	8	1	5	6	9
6	4	7	1	2	8	9	5	3
9	5	8	7	4	3	6	1	2
1	3	2	6	5	9	4	8	7

SUDOKU - 37 (Solution)

6	4	9	2	1	7	5	8	3
2	8	3	9	4	5	7	6	1
1	7	5	3	8	6	4	9	2
9	1	7	8	2	3	6	4	5
3	6	8	4	5	9	1	2	7
5	2	4	7	6	1	8	3	9
4	5	6	1	9	2	3	7	8
7	9	1	6	3	8	2	5	4
8	3	2	5	7	4	9	1	6

SUDOKU - 38 (Solution)

4	8	7	2	6	1	5	9	3
6	1	3	7	5	9	2	8	4
5	2	9	8	3	4	6	1	7
2	7	1	5	9	3	8	4	6
8	3	6	1	4	2	7	5	9
9	5	4	6	7	8	1	3	2
7	9	5	4	1	6	3	2	8
1	4	2	3	8	7	9	6	5
3	6	8	9	2	5	4	7	1

SUDOKU - 43 (Solution)

3	7	4	6	5	2	9	8	1
2	5	6	8	1	9	4	7	3
9	8	1	3	7	4	5	2	6
7	3	5	2	4	8	1	6	9
6	4	9	7	3	1	2	5	8
8	1	2	5	9	6	3	4	7
1	9	8	4	6	5	7	3	2
4	2	3	9	8	7	6	1	5
5	6	7	1	2	3	8	9	4

SUDOKU - 44 (Solution)

2	6	3	1	4	7	8	9	5
5	8	9	6	3	2	1	7	4
7	4	1	9	8	5	2	3	6
3	5	7	4	1	6	9	8	2
1	9	4	7	2	8	5	6	3
6	2	8	3	5	9	4	1	7
9	3	2	8	7	4	6	5	1
4	7	6	5	9	1	3	2	8
8	1	5	2	6	3	7	4	9

SUDOKU - 39 (Solution)

6	1	3	5	2	8	7	4	9
2	7	4	9	3	6	5	1	8
9	8	5	4	7	1	3	6	2
5	2	6	3	4	9	1	8	7
7	4	1	2	8	5	6	9	3
3	9	8	6	1	7	2	5	4
4	3	9	1	6	2	8	7	5
1	5	7	8	9	3	4	2	6
8	6	2	7	5	4	9	3	1

SUDOKU - 40 (Solution)

9	3	6	7	1	5	4	2	8
5	7	1	4	8	2	6	9	3
4	8	2	3	9	6	7	5	1
2	5	7	1	3	8	9	6	4
3	6	4	9	2	7	8	1	5
1	9	8	6	5	4	3	7	2
8	4	5	2	6	9	1	3	7
6	2	3	8	7	1	5	4	9
7	1	9	5	4	3	2	8	6

SUDOKU - 45 (Solution)

7	4	2	6	8	3	1	9	5
1	9	3	7	4	5	8	2	6
6	8	5	2	9	1	3	7	4
2	7	1	9	6	4	5	3	8
9	5	4	8	3	2	7	6	1
3	6	8	5	1	7	2	4	9
5	3	6	1	7	9	4	8	2
8	2	7	4	5	6	9	1	3
4	1	9	3	2	8	6	5	7

SUDOKU - 46 (Solution)

4	5	2	9	6	8	3	1	7
8	7	1	5	3	2	4	9	6
9	6	3	4	1	7	5	8	2
1	9	8	2	5	6	7	3	4
3	2	7	8	4	9	1	6	5
5	4	6	3	7	1	8	2	9
6	3	9	7	8	4	2	5	1
2	8	4	1	9	5	6	7	3
7	1	5	6	2	3	9	4	8

SUDOKU - 41 (Solution)

2	1	3	9	7	6	4	5	8
5	6	4	2	1	8	3	7	9
7	9	8	3	5	4	1	6	2
8	5	2	7	6	1	9	4	3
4	3	6	5	2	9	8	1	7
1	7	9	4	8	3	5	2	6
3	8	7	6	4	5	2	9	1
6	4	1	8	9	2	7	3	5
9	2	5	1	3	7	6	8	4

SUDOKU - 42 (Solution)

3	5	8	1	7	9	2	4	6
7	4	6	2	8	3	1	5	9
1	2	9	4	6	5	3	8	7
6	8	1	3	2	7	5	9	4
9	3	4	8	5	6	7	2	1
2	7	5	9	1	4	6	3	8
4	6	2	7	3	8	9	1	5
8	1	7	5	9	2	4	6	3
5	9	3	6	4	1	8	7	2

SUDOKU - 47 (Solution)

5	9	1	4	3	8	2	6	7
7	2	3	5	9	6	1	4	8
4	8	6	2	7	1	5	3	9
8	7	4	9	1	5	6	2	3
6	1	2	8	4	3	9	7	5
3	5	9	6	2	7	8	1	4
9	3	7	1	5	2	4	8	6
1	6	5	3	8	4	7	9	2
2	4	8	7	6	9	3	5	1

SUDOKU - 48 (Solution)

4	7	9	6	3	1	2	5	8
6	8	2	9	5	7	1	3	4
5	3	1	8	4	2	7	6	9
7	9	3	5	6	8	4	1	2
8	1	4	3	2	9	6	7	5
2	6	5	7	1	4	9	8	3
9	5	6	4	7	3	8	2	1
1	4	7	2	8	5	3	9	6
3	2	8	1	9	6	5	4	7

SUDOKU - 49 (Solution)

8	9	6	4	2	1	7	3	5
5	3	7	6	9	8	2	1	4
2	4	1	3	5	7	6	9	8
9	6	2	7	1	4	8	5	3
7	8	3	9	6	5	1	4	2
1	5	4	2	8	3	9	7	6
3	1	5	8	7	2	4	6	9
4	2	9	1	3	6	5	8	7
6	7	8	5	4	9	3	2	1

SUDOKU - 50 (Solution)

7	2	4	6	1	8	9	3	5
8	9	6	3	4	5	2	7	1
3	1	5	9	7	2	6	8	4
2	6	8	7	3	4	1	5	9
9	3	1	2	5	6	7	4	8
5	4	7	1	8	9	3	2	6
4	7	9	5	2	1	8	6	3
1	8	2	4	6	3	5	9	7
6	5	3	8	9	7	4	1	2

SUDOKU - 55 (Solution)

8	3	6	5	2	7	9	1	4
1	2	7	3	9	4	8	5	6
4	9	5	6	8	1	3	7	2
2	1	8	7	4	5	6	3	9
6	5	4	8	3	9	7	2	1
9	7	3	2	1	6	5	4	8
3	6	9	4	5	2	1	8	7
5	4	1	9	7	8	2	6	3
7	8	2	1	6	3	4	9	5

SUDOKU - 56 (Solution)

3	5	2	9	6	8	1	7	4
4	8	7	5	1	3	2	6	9
6	1	9	7	4	2	5	3	8
9	4	1	2	7	5	3	8	6
7	6	5	8	3	4	9	1	2
2	3	8	1	9	6	7	4	5
1	7	6	4	2	9	8	5	3
5	2	3	6	8	1	4	9	7
8	9	4	3	5	7	6	2	1

SUDOKU - 51 (Solution)

5	2	7	1	8	4	3	9	6
6	8	4	2	3	9	5	7	1
9	1	3	6	5	7	8	2	4
2	4	8	7	1	3	6	5	9
1	7	5	4	9	6	2	3	8
3	9	6	5	2	8	1	4	7
4	5	1	9	6	2	7	8	3
7	3	2	8	4	1	9	6	5
8	6	9	3	7	5	4	1	2

SUDOKU - 52 (Solution)

2	4	8	7	3	9	5	6	1
3	7	9	5	6	1	4	2	8
5	6	1	2	4	8	7	9	3
1	3	6	4	9	5	2	8	7
4	5	2	3	8	7	9	1	6
8	9	7	1	2	6	3	5	4
6	2	5	8	7	3	1	4	9
7	8	4	9	1	2	6	3	5
9	1	3	6	5	4	8	7	2

SUDOKU - 57 (Solution)

6	1	3	4	9	2	5	8	7
9	8	2	3	7	5	6	4	1
4	5	7	8	6	1	9	2	3
8	7	4	9	2	3	1	5	6
2	6	1	5	8	7	4	3	9
3	9	5	6	1	4	8	7	2
5	4	9	7	3	6	2	1	8
7	2	6	1	4	8	3	9	5
1	3	8	2	5	9	7	6	4

SUDOKU - 58 (Solution)

2	3	7	9	8	5	6	1	4
5	9	6	1	7	4	3	8	2
4	8	1	2	3	6	5	7	9
9	7	8	5	2	3	4	6	1
3	1	5	4	6	7	2	9	8
6	2	4	8	1	9	7	5	3
7	6	9	3	4	1	8	2	5
1	4	2	7	5	8	9	3	6
8	5	3	6	9	2	1	4	7

SUDOKU - 53 (Solution)

3	1	9	2	6	5	4	7	8
2	7	4	3	8	9	1	5	6
8	5	6	1	7	4	3	9	2
4	3	5	6	1	8	7	2	9
7	6	1	5	9	2	8	4	3
9	8	2	4	3	7	5	6	1
1	9	3	7	5	6	2	8	4
6	2	7	8	4	3	9	1	5
5	4	8	9	2	1	6	3	7

SUDOKU - 54 (Solution)

3	2	1	5	4	8	7	9	6
9	7	4	6	3	2	1	8	5
6	5	8	7	9	1	2	3	4
8	6	2	4	5	7	3	1	9
4	9	3	8	1	6	5	2	7
7	1	5	9	2	3	4	6	8
5	3	7	1	6	9	8	4	2
1	4	6	2	8	5	9	7	3
2	8	9	3	7	4	6	5	1

SUDOKU - 59 (Solution)

1	8	7	6	9	3	4	2	5
3	6	5	4	2	7	9	8	1
9	4	2	1	5	8	7	6	3
6	3	9	7	4	5	8	1	2
7	1	4	2	8	6	3	5	9
5	2	8	3	1	9	6	7	4
4	5	3	8	6	2	1	9	7
2	7	6	9	3	1	5	4	8
8	9	1	5	7	4	2	3	6

SUDOKU - 60 (Solution)

2	5	4	7	3	1	6	8	9
3	7	6	5	8	9	1	4	2
8	1	9	6	4	2	7	3	5
4	6	3	8	9	7	2	5	1
9	2	5	4	1	6	8	7	3
1	8	7	3	2	5	4	9	6
5	3	1	2	7	8	9	6	4
6	9	8	1	5	4	3	2	7
7	4	2	9	6	3	5	1	8

CROSSWORD

CROSSWORD Puzzle : 1
```
LARD  ATOM  CHE
ILIA  LONE  HAW
EBBS  GROG  ICE
    YUAN  RACKS
NATURE  PIN
YEARN  DIM  AAH
ERNE  CAP  FILE
TOG  QOM  OLDER
   BUS  PAUSED
HIREE  SOFT
IDO  ELUL  ISLE
TOP  NARY  SPOT
SLY  SWAP  TATA
```

CROSSWORD Puzzle : 2
```
FUMY  ROTA  DDT
ESAU  EGOS  IOU
WALL  AERY  NUB
   ERIE  LIEGE
DOLLAR  BUN
IDIOM  LAM  BOY
MOOG  OUD  FARE
ERN  LAX  URBAN
   ILK  TRIALS
TESTA  AONE
ODA  MASK  NOOK
GAM  ARIA  DICE
AMP  STAY  SLAG
```

CROSSWORD Puzzle : 3
```
LACY  VOID  GIB
ACHE  AARE  LOO
BEER  UREA  ITS
    EELS  CUBAN
CRAVAT  COP
RABAT  NON  PAS
EVEN  SIB  SECT
EEL  CUP  PIANO
   GAR  TINSEL
BIJOU  RANK
ODA  DOUR  EARP
YET  ACER  ROAR
SAO  LADY  SKYE
```

CROSSWORD Puzzle : 4
```
PIGS  IRKS  KEF
URAL  NAIL  ODA
NEMO  UPDO  JAG
   WAIT  SWIMS
ASSERT  THE
AMUSE  NAY  RYA
RUNT  IOU  MEOW
EGG  LOT  TINGE
   BON  HALOID
TINEA  SAIL
OLE  DOHS  ETNA
FIR  EBON  ROAR
FAD  RIOT  STEM
```

CROSSWORD Puzzle : 5
```
HAND  MYNA  CAM
IYAR  AEON  OCA
SEMI  NUNS  CHI
   BASK  WAKEN
SOMBRE  BEN
WHALE  JAR  IDO
AIDE  MAR  WREN
POE  FEY  BRIBE
   PAL  BOASTS
SERIC  MOAN
IVE  ILEX  GALE
NIL  LASE  LIEF
SLY  EYAS  EMIT
```

CROSSWORD Puzzle : 6
```
SOBS  CHEW  SEE
WRAP  LURE  ALT
YETI  ALEE  GUT
   NASA  DHOLE
CROUCH  DEE
AISLE  BID  LIT
ELLE  WAD  PESO
NEO  GAR  COALS
   HUN  FISHES
QUAIL  OLDS
ARC  LAVA  EPEE
DIM  EXAM  SLOT
ICE  TELE  SYNC
```

CROSSWORD Puzzle : 7
```
FEND  FOIN  WAN
ILIA  OLLA  ERE
NIPS  LIEN  REE
   HALO  SWEAR
GRAINY  BEE
HANKY  SUN  LOG
ANTI  JET  PERI
TIA  KEA  NAWAB
   MAW  GIRDLE
CHEEK  HULK
UEY  ABUT  IBIS
PAR  PIGS  NINA
SPA  OBEY  GONG
```

CROSSWORD Puzzle : 8
```
TALA  NETT  EGO
AGES  OAHU  YON
VENT  ICES  ROC
   RASH  CHAFE
PUMICE  LAE
SPADE  EON  URB
SOLE  GAB  TRIO
TNT  MAR  MODEL
   OUD  PAPULE
FRANC  SACK
AIR  OAKS  NOEL
CAM  UTAH  OWES
ELY  SETA  TEND
```

CROSSWORD Puzzle : 9
```
CINE  GOAD  COG
EDAM  UMBO  OLE
TOGO  NICE  PIN
   TENT  SUEDE
GRAINY  INS
EARNS  CAT  CAP
AGOG  RIM  TOPE
RAW  LED  RAISE
   SUE  BARREL
CAROB  AAHS
USA  BULL  INLY
SEN  EGOS  EASE
PAD  RHEA  REDS
```

CROSSWORD Puzzle : 10
```
FRAU  SWAB  GAM
EARL  QADI  ISA
EMMY  URSA  ZAP
   SCAM  SNAPS
SOUSED  GEO
ONSET  KID  SAC
ACES  TET  LOBE
PED  OAF  DICED
   DDT  LEGATE
STOOD  BERN
WAR  ELLE  IRAN
OCA  SOAK  TIRE
TOD  TOES  EPEE
```

CROSSWORD Puzzle : 11
```
POSE  AEON  JUS
EVEN  LINO  USE
GAEA  ORES  JEW
   MOUE  INURN
THREAD  ONO
BAULK  HOG  TON
ARES  OAF  POLE
RED  KID  BRUIT
   DAL  BOARDS
JACOB  AONE
IDA  UNDO  TAPS
VAN  KIDS  OVAL
EMS  INST  RELY
```

CROSSWORD Puzzle : 12
```
HENT  SYCE  SHE
OGEE  PEEL  NOD
TOTE  LUTE  ORE
   TEAK  CUBAN
UPSHOT  ITS
PALES  COS  ARC
OVER  NAN  OBIE
NED  PAW  PLEAD
   MAY  FUDDLE
SPEEL  ALPS
AID  LUXE  HUES
NEG  ISIS  OSLO
ERE  DASH  EELS
```

CROSSWORD Puzzle : 13
```
FUME  STAB  ZIP
IRON  OHIO  ERR
TBAR  PELT  TEA
   AVON  TOADY
BADGER  TEN
AGREE  MES  JAG
CRUS  KID  SAGE
HAG  SEX  OLEUM
   SEA  ANELES
DEMOS  UPON
ICE  ALPS  DOHS
ERA  MADE  EPEE
TUN  EGOS  RENT
```

CROSSWORD Puzzle : 14
```
EARN  BALD  DUD
PLEA  OGEE  END
ITEM  URAL  VIA
   EYRA  UNITY
SEADOG  IDO
ILIAD  POE  REP
VARY  FLU  ROLL
ANY  PAY  TEASE
   AID  SUBDEB
LENTO  ULNA
ORE  LYRE  TROT
RIO  EASE  EURO
EEN  THAT  DEBT
```

CROSSWORD Puzzle : 15
```
JIGS  ALAR  ALB
URAL  BONE  NAE
GETA  BLIP  IVE
   NOEL  ATLAS
MIDDAY  BIO
UDDER  POD  SOU
SEAR  HOG  TOGS
SAY  BIP  GILES
   GYP  WANDER
SCOOP  HASH
HEY  AVID  ORGY
IDE  SAFE  RHEA
VIZ  STIR  NONG
```

CROSSWORD Puzzle : 16
```
TIRE  SWAG  KEA
ASAP  TAIL  NAP
BATS  AFRO  EVE
   ISNT  VOWED
COILED  PEN
AARON  GAS  NUT
THEN  GAL  SARI
OUD  YIP  SERGE
   MAG  SOCCER
TAKEN  SALE
UZI  QUOD  DAWN
NAN  URAL  EPEE
END  INKY  DEBT
```

CROSSWORD Puzzle : 17
```
GURU  CEDE  RID
AZAN  UPDO  ANI
BIPS  LETS  ITS
   NAPE  IONIC
NEVADA  INK
OVERS  COS  DAL
SELL  YIN  GOBI
END  TAD  URGER
   NEG  EGESTA
GENOA  ASHY
RIO  MOCK  HISS
URN  ERNE  ERIE
BEE  DEER  NENE
```

CROSSWORD Puzzle : 18
```
PIET  HARD  EMS
LORE  APIA  REE
YUAN  BEDE  GAR
   ARID  DHOLE
COMBAT  TAE
ADULT  SOL  JAR
LODE  PUG  TUBA
MRS  LAE  LABEL
   GUN  AERATE
CAROB  ERIN
ELI  BALT  IAGO
ILL  ERSE  SNUB
LYE  REEF  HITS
```

CROSSWORD Puzzle : 19
```
KLAN  LASS  ACT
EURO  ACHE  DOR
AGES  RHEA  IDA
   ENVY  SATAY
ZAMBIA  ION
AXIAL  PAN  BRA
MING  SUM  TOUR
ASK  TAT  PAINT
   NAN  HURLEY
PECOS  SAPS
ORE  SOTS  INTI
KIN  EBON  EARN
EST  LILT  REIN
```

CROSSWORD Puzzle : 20
```
NEMO  REEL  RHO
AYES  EPEE  HOP
EELS  IONS  ERE
   EGGS  ISAAC
LAGOON  LOO
ABOUT  NIN  AWL
DEBS  LYE  TRIO
ELI  SIX  HAIFA
   BIP  RIDDED
SPEEL  SEEP
CAT  ASKS  OMIT
ULT  GAEA  LEAH
TEE  EDGY  EMMY
```

ABC PATH

ABC PATH - 1 (Solution)
```
22 11 10 23  8  5 12
18 │16 18 19  1  3│  3
15 │15 17 20  2  4│ 20
25 │14 24 25 21  5│ 24
 6 │11 13 23 22  6│ 13
 9 │12 10  9  8  7│  7
 2 14 17 19 21  4 16
```

ABC PATH - 2 (Solution)
```
10  7 16 12 22  2  6
11 │10 11 15 14 25│ 15
13 │ 9 16 12 13 24│  9
23 │ 8 17 18 22 23│ 17
20 │ 7 19 20 21  1│ 19
 3 │ 6  5  4  3  2│  4
25  8  5 18 14 24 21
```

ABC PATH - 7 (Solution)
```
 4 10  7  6 20  3 17
15 │12 13 15 16 17│ 16
14 │11 14 24  1 18│ 24
23 │10 23 25 19  2│  2
 9 │ 9 22 21 20  3│ 22
 5 │ 8  7  6  5  4│  8
25 11 13 21 19 18 12
```

ABC PATH - 8 (Solution)
```
24  2  4 18 16 19 20
13 │12 13 14 16 17│ 17
10 │11 10 15 20 18│ 15
 3 │ 3  9  8 21 19│  9
23 │ 2  4  7 22 23│ 22
 6 │ 1  5  6 25 24│ 25
17 11  5  7 21 18  8
```

ABC PATH - 3 (Solution)
```
22 16 20 18  3  5 12
17 │16 17 23 24 25│ 24
15 │15 22 18  3  2│  2
 4 │14 21 19  1  4│ 21
13 │13 20  8  9  5│  8
10 │12 11 10  7  6│  7
19 14 11 23  9 25  6
```

ABC PATH - 4 (Solution)
```
24 10 13 15 25 19  7
17 │11 12 15 16 17│ 12
14 │10 13 14 18 19│ 18
 2 │ 9  2  1 25 20│  9
21 │ 8  3  4 24 21│  4
22 │ 7  6  5 23 22│ 23
 3  8  6 16 20 11
```

ABC PATH - 9 (Solution)
```
 9 16 20  4  3  7  3
19 │19 20 22 23 25│ 22
11 │18 21 11 10 24│ 18
 6 │17 12  9  6  7│ 12
 8 │16 13  5  8  1│ 13
15 │15 14  4  3  2│  2
10 17 14  5 23 24 21
```

ABC PATH - 10 (Solution)
```
20  2 21 18 19 15 12
 6 │ 5  6  7 11 12│ 11
13 │ 4  8  9 10 13│  9
14 │ 3 21 20 19 14│  3
17 │ 2 22 18 17 15│ 22
23 │ 1 23 24 25 16│ 24
10  4  8  7 25 16  5
```

ABC PATH - 5 (Solution)
```
18  5  4 13 22 20 25
10 │ 6  7  8  9 10│  7
11 │ 5  4  3  2 11│  3
16 │16 17 18 12  1│ 12
14 │15 14 13 19 20│ 15
23 │25 24 23 22 21│ 24
 2  6 17  8  9 21 19
```

ABC PATH - 6 (Solution)
```
25  7 20 22 23 13 19
 9 │ 7  8  9 10 11│ 11
 5 │ 5  6 22 23 12│ 12
21 │ 4 20 21 24 13│ 24
 3 │ 3 19 18 25 14│ 18
15 │ 2  1 17 16 15│ 16
 2  4  8 17 10 14  6
```

ABC PATH - 11 (Solution)
```
17 16 13 18 10  7 22
 5 │ 1  2  3  4  5│  3
19 │25 17 18 19  6│ 25
24 │16 24 22 20  7│ 20
23 │23 21 12 21  8│  8
11 │14 13 11 10  9│  9
14 15  2 12  4  6 21
```

ABC PATH - 12 (Solution)
```
15  4 16  7 10 20  9
17 │15 16 17 18 19│ 18
11 │14 13 12 11 20│ 13
 2 │ 3  2  9 10 21│ 21
22 │ 4  1  8 23 22│ 22
 5 │ 5  6  7 24 25│ 24
19 14  6 12 23 21 25
```

ABC PATH - 13 (Solution)
```
10 17 13 20  8  3  6
18 │18 19 20  1  2│  2
22 │17 22 21  5  3│ 21
23 │23 16  6  8  4│ 16
 9 │15 24 25  7  9│ 25
14 │14 13 12 11 10│ 11
24 15 19 12  5  4  7
```

ABC PATH - 14 (Solution)
```
25 13 11 10 24  4  2
20 │19 20 21  1  2│ 21
18 │18 17 22 23  3│  3
16 │14 16 25 24  4│ 14
 8 │13 15  9  8  5│  9
 7 │12 11 10  7  6│ 12
15 19 17 22 23  5  6
```

ABC PATH - 19 (Solution)
```
 8 17 10 21 12 25 23
19 │19 20 21 22 24│ 24
18 │18  8  7 23 25│  7
 9 │17  9  6  1  2│  2
 5 │16 10 13  5  3│ 13
14 │15 14 11 12  4│ 15
 6 16 20 11 22  3  4
```

ABC PATH - 20 (Solution)
```
22 19 21 24  6  5  4
20 │20 21  7  6  5│  5
 8 │19 22  8  4  2│  2
18 │18 23  9  1  3│  3
17 │17 25 24 10 11│ 10
15 │16 15 14 13 12│ 14
25 16 23  9 13 11 12
```

ABC PATH - 15 (Solution)
```
25 10  7 15 16 18 17
14 │13 14 15 16 17│ 13
23 │12 22 23 24 18│ 12
21 │11 21 25 19  1│ 11
20 │10  7 20  4  2│  4
 5 │ 9  8  6  5  3│  8
24  9 22  6 19  2  3
```

ABC PATH - 16 (Solution)
```
25 13 11 10 24  4  2
20 │19 20 21  1  2│ 21
18 │18 17 22 23  3│  3
16 │14 16 25 24  4│ 14
 8 │13 15  9  8  5│  9
 7 │12 11 10  7  6│ 12
15 19 17 22 23  5  6
```

ABC PATH - 21 (Solution)
```
24  3 18 17 22 14 10
 7 │ 6  7  8  9 10│  9
11 │ 5 19 20 21 11│ 20
12 │ 4 18 24 22 12│  4
23 │ 3 25 17 23 13│ 25
16 │ 2  1 16 15 14│ 14
21  5 19  8 15 13  6
```

ABC PATH - 22 (Solution)
```
 2 13  7 22 21 19  9
16 │13 14 15 16 17│ 14
25 │12 25 22 21 18│ 12
24 │11 24 23 20 19│ 20
10 │10  7  6  5  1│  6
 4 │ 9  8  4  3  2│  2
17 11  8 15  5 18 23
```

ABC PATH - 17 (Solution)
```
22  4 21 25 18 14 12
 7 │ 7  8  9 10 12│  9
11 │ 6 22 23 11 13│  6
24 │ 5 21 25 24 14│  5
15 │ 4 20 19 16 15│ 19
17 │ 3  2  1 18 17│  2
20  3  8 23 10 13 16
```

ABC PATH - 18 (Solution)
```
 7 17 19 20  8  5 11
 2 │18 19 20  2  1│ 18
21 │17 16 21  3  4│ 16
25 │13 15 22 25  5│ 22
12 │12 14 23 24  6│  6
10 │11 10  9  8  7│  9
14 13 15 23  3  4 24
```

ABC PATH - 23 (Solution)
```
 3  2 17 16  6 10 18
 4 │ 2  4  5  6  7│  7
23 │ 1  3 23  9  8│  9
24 │21 22 25 24 10│ 25
11 │20 18 16 15 11│ 20
14 │19 17 14 13 12│ 12
19 21 22  5 13  8 15
```

ABC PATH - 24 (Solution)
```
20 19 17 22  8  2  9
23 │20 21 22 23  1│ 21
24 │19 18 25 24  2│ 25
16 │16 17  9  8  3│  3
12 │15 12 10  7  4│ 10
 6 │14 13 11  6  5│  5
14 15 13 11  7  4 18
```

ABC PATH - 25 (Solution)

```
 7   4   6  10  11  13  23
 9 | 7   9  10  11  12 | 12
25 | 8   6  25  15  13 | 15
 5 | 5  24  23  16  14 | 16
17 | 4  22  21  19  17 | 22
18 | 3   2   1  20  18 |  2
 3   8  24  21  20  14  19
```

ABC PATH - 26 (Solution)

```
25  22  20  10  13  15  21
12 | 8   9  10  11  12 |  8
 4 | 7   4   3  13  14 |  3
 6 | 6   5   2   1  15 |  5
16 |22  23  24  25  16 | 24
17 |21  20  19  18  17 | 18
23   7   9  19  11  14   2
```

ABC PATH - 31 (Solution)

```
 4   2   3  23  24  17  14
10 | 9  10  11  12  14 | 12
13 | 8   6   5  15  13 |  5
16 | 7   3   4  24  16 |  7
25 | 2  21  23  25  17 | 21
22 | 1  22  20  19  18 | 20
15   8   6  11  19  18   9
```

ABC PATH - 32 (Solution)

```
23   6   2   8   9  11  18
 7 | 6   7   8   9  10 | 10
 4 | 5   4   3  25  11 | 25
12 | 1   2  21  24  12 | 24
19 |19  20  22  23  13 | 22
17 |18  17  16  15  14 | 16
21   5  20   3  15  13  14
```

ABC PATH - 27 (Solution)

```
23   5  11  10  13  15  14
 9 | 8   9  10  13  14 |  8
12 | 7  11  12  24  15 | 24
 6 | 6  22  23  25  16 | 25
17 | 5   2  21  19  17 |  2
18 | 4   3   1  20  18 |  3
 4   7  22  21  20  16  19
```

ABC PATH - 28 (Solution)

```
20   5  21   2  15  25  16
24 |20  21  22  23  24 | 22
18 |19  18  17  16  25 | 17
14 | 5   4   3  15  14 |  4
11 | 6   1   2  11  13 |  6
12 | 7   8   9  10  12 | 10
 7  19   8   9  23  13   3
```

ABC PATH - 33 (Solution)

```
18  24  11  17   2   8  25
15 |15  16   1   2   3 |  3
14 |14  18  17   4   5 |  5
20 |13  23  19  20   6 | 23
 7 |24  12  22  21   7 | 22
 9 |25  11  10   9   8 | 10
12  13  16  19   4   6  21
```

ABC PATH - 34 (Solution)

```
13  17  20  22   6   7   9
 4 | 3   4   5   6   7 |  5
21 | 2  21  22   9   8 |  8
23 | 1  20  23  10  11 | 10
18 |18  19  24  25  12 | 12
15 |17  16  15  14  13 | 14
19   2  16  24  25  11   3
```

ABC PATH - 29 (Solution)

```
 5  10  25  18  23  22   8
20 |14  15  16  17  20 | 16
21 |11  13  18  19  21 | 11
12 |10  12  24  23  22 | 24
 9 | 9  25   6   5   1 |  6
 3 | 8   7   4   3   2 |  7
19  14  15   4  17   2  13
```

ABC PATH - 30 (Solution)

```
 6  18  11  21  24   3  25
19 |19  20  21   1   2 |  2
17 |18  17  22  23   3 | 22
14 |14  16  25  24   4 | 16
 5 |13  15   9   8   5 |  9
12 |12  11  10   7   6 |  9
15  13  20  10  23   4   8
```

ABC PATH - 35 (Solution)

```
15  25   3   5  19  10  11
 2 | 2   3   5   7   8 |  8
 6 | 1   4   6  11   9 |  9
12 |25  14  15  12  10 | 14
16 |23  24  13  16  17 | 13
21 |22  21  20  19  18 | 18
22  23  24  20   7  17   4
```

ABC PATH - 36 (Solution)

```
25  11   4  14  23  19   5
18 |12  13  14  17  18 | 13
16 |11  10  15  16  19 | 10
 7 | 7   9  25  22  20 | 22
24 | 6   8  24  23  21 | 21
 3 | 5   4   3   2   1 |  2
 8   6   9  15  17  20  12
```

ABC PATH - 37 (Solution)

```
24  10  11  12  25  19  17
13 |10  11  12  13  18 | 18
14 | 9  15  14  17  19 |  9
 7 | 8   7  16  25  20 | 20
 2 | 6   1   2  24  21 |  6
 4 | 5   4   3  23  22 |  3
 5   8  15  16  23  21  22
```

ABC PATH - 38 (Solution)

```
 4  17  25  24   7  22  13
19 |17  18  19  20  21 | 18
23 |16  25  24  23  22 | 16
 9 |15   9  10   1   2 |  2
14 |14  11   8   7   3 | 11
 6 |13  12   6   5   4 |  5
21  15  12   8  20   3  10
```

ABC PATH - 43 (Solution)

```
12   9   5  20  25  15   6
14 |10  11  13  14  15 | 11
24 | 9  12  24  25  16 | 16
18 | 8  23  21  18  17 |  8
 7 | 7  22  20  19   1 | 19
 2 | 6   5   4   3   2 |  4
22  10  23  13   3  17  21
```

ABC PATH - 44 (Solution)

```
 4  10   7   3  25  20  16
14 |12  13  14  15  16 | 13
17 |11   4   3   2  17 | 11
 5 |10   5   1  24  18 | 24
 9 | 9   6  23  25  19 | 19
21 | 8   7  22  21  20 | 22
 2   8   6  23  15  18  12
```

ABC PATH - 39 (Solution)

```
 4  23   7   8  10  15   3
 9 | 6   7   9  10  11 |  6
 5 | 5   4   8   1  12 | 12
 2 |23  24   3   2  13 | 13
20 |22  20  25  14  15 | 25
21 |21  19  18  17  16 | 19
11  22  24  18  17  16  14
```

ABC PATH - 40 (Solution)

```
25   5  19  18  23  14   3
 9 | 7   8   9  10  11 |  7
21 | 6  21  22  23  12 | 12
24 | 5  20  25  24  13 | 20
17 | 4  19  18  17  14 |  4
16 | 3   2   1  16  15 |  2
11   6   8  22  10  13  15
```

ABC PATH - 45 (Solution)

```
21  10  11   6  25  17  15
12 |10  11  12  14  15 | 14
16 | 9   7  13  16  17 | 13
 5 | 8   5   6  18  19 |  8
20 | 2   4  24  25  20 |  2
23 | 1   3  23  22  21 | 22
 4   9   3  24  18  19   7
```

ABC PATH - 46 (Solution)

```
23  22   9   7   2  14  10
24 |23  24   7   6   5 |  6
 8 |22  25   8   2   4 | 25
11 |21   9  11   3   1 |  3
13 |20  10  12  13  14 | 20
19 |19  18  17  16  15 | 17
 5  21  18  12  16   4  15
```

ABC PATH - 41 (Solution)

```
25  11   9  15   7   4  10
20 |19  20  21   1   2 |  2
18 |18  17  23  22   3 | 23
16 |13  12  16  24   4 | 12
 5 |11  14  15  25   5 | 14
 8 |10   9   8   7   6 |  6
22  13  17  21  24   3  19
```

ABC PATH - 42 (Solution)

```
24  10   9  13  18  16  15
14 |11  12  13  14  15 | 12
17 |10   9  25  17  16 | 25
 7 | 8   7  24  18  19 |  8
 3 | 3   2   6  23  20 | 20
22 | 1   4   5  22  21 |  5
 2  11   4   6  23  19  21
```

ABC PATH - 47 (Solution)

```
 2  22  20   4  14  11  21
 7 | 2   3   4   7   8 |  8
10 | 1   5   6   9  10 |  6
13 |23  24  25  13  11 | 24
18 |22  18  19  14  12 | 19
17 |21  20  17  16  15 | 15
 9  23   3  25  16  12   5
```

ABC PATH - 48 (Solution)

```
 4   5  10  14  22  19  13
17 | 1   2  15  16  17 | 15
25 | 3   4  14  25  18 |  3
 6 | 5   6  13  24  19 | 24
 7 | 8   7  12  23  20 | 20
11 | 9  10  11  22  21 | 21
 9   8   2  12  16  18  23
```

ABC PATH - 49 (Solution)

```
14  7 10 16  4 25  9
19 |14 15 16 18 19| 18
17 |13 11 17 24 20| 13
21 |12 10 23 21 25| 12
 3 | 8  9 22  3  2|  2
 5 | 7  6  5  4  1|  6
23  8 15 22 24 20 11
```

ABC PATH - 50 (Solution)

```
 2 12 23 14  3 17 16
13 |12 13 14 15 16| 15
24 |11 23 24 25 17| 11
19 | 8 10 22 19 18| 10
20 | 7  9 21 20  1|  7
 4 | 6  5  4  3  2|  5
 6  8  9 21 25 18 22
```

ABC PATH - 55 (Solution)

```
21  3  9 10 22 18 13
11 | 7  8 10 11 12|  8
15 | 6  9 15 13 17| 17
 5 | 5 25 14 16 18| 25
23 | 4 24 23 22 19|  4
 2 | 3  2  1 20 21| 20
12  6 24 14 16 19  7
```

ABC PATH - 56 (Solution)

```
14  6 21 16 24 13 10
 8 | 6  7  8  9 10|  7
25 | 5 20 19 25 11| 20
 4 | 4 21 18 24 12| 12
22 | 3 17 22 23 13|  3
15 | 2  1 16 15 14| 14
18  5 17 19  9 11 23
```

ABC PATH - 51 (Solution)

```
24 19  3 16  5 11  6
 4 | 2  3  4  5  6|  2
 7 |22  1  8  7 10| 10
23 |21 23 24  9 11| 21
25 |19 20 25 12 13| 20
14 |18 17 16 15 14| 15
18 22 17  8  9 13 12
```

ABC PATH - 52 (Solution)

```
14  2  7  8 25 10 23
 9 | 6  7  8  9 10|  6
 5 | 5 21 22 23 11| 11
12 | 4 19 20 24 12|  4
18 | 3 18 17 25 13| 17
15 | 2  1 16 15 14| 16
20  3 19 22 24 13 21
```

ABC PATH - 57 (Solution)

```
10 17 22  2 24  7 14
 3 |20 21  3  4  5| 21
 6 |19 22  2  1  6| 19
18 |16 18 23 24  7| 23
 8 |17 15 25  8  9|  9
11 |14 13 12 11 10| 12
15 16 13 25  4  5 20
```

ABC PATH - 58 (Solution)

```
23 15 11 22  3  5 12
 4 |16 17  2  3  4|  2
25 |15 18  1 25  5| 18
19 |14 19 20 24  6| 24
13 |13 21 22 23  7|  7
 8 |12 11 10  9  8| 10
21 14 17 20  9  6 16
```

ABC PATH - 53 (Solution)

```
12  9  5  4 24 20 15
11 |10 11 23 24 25| 23
21 | 9 12 14 22 21| 14
18 | 8 13 15 18 20|  8
19 | 7 16 17 19  2| 16
 6 | 6  5  4  3  1|  3
25  7 13 17 22  2 10
```

ABC PATH - 54 (Solution)

```
14  6  7 22 24 13 10
 8 | 6  7  8  9 10|  9
20 | 5 20 19 25 11| 25
12 | 4 21 18 24 12|  4
 3 | 3 17 22 23 13| 23
16 | 2  1 16 15 14|  2
17  5 21 19 15 11 18
```

ABC PATH - 59 (Solution)

```
 9  6  7 16 10 20  4
15 |14 15 16 18 19| 18
17 | 2 13 12 17 20|  2
11 | 3  1  9 11 21| 21
 8 | 6  4  8 10 22| 22
25 | 5  7 25 24 23| 23
 5  3 13 12 24 19 14
```

ABC PATH - 60 (Solution)

```
21 14 17 18  9  7  8
10 |13 11 10  9  8| 11
12 |14 12  2  1  7|  2
 3 |15  3  4  5  6| 15
16 |16 17 18 19 20| 20
23 |25 24 23 22 21| 22
25 13 24  4  5  6 19
```

MAZES

Intermediate
MAZE - 1

Intermediate
MAZE - 2

Intermediate
MAZE - 3

Intermediate
MAZE - 4

MAZE - 5

MAZE - 6

MAZE - 7

MAZE - 8

MAZE - 9

MAZE - 10

MAZE - 11

Solutions

KRISSKROSS

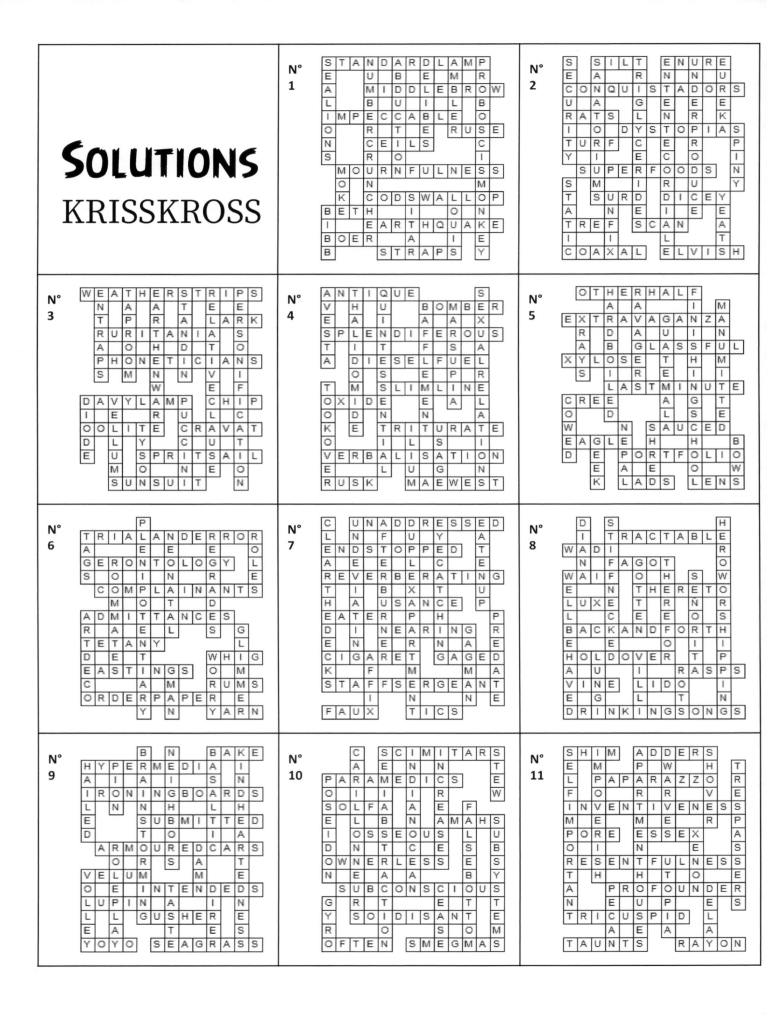

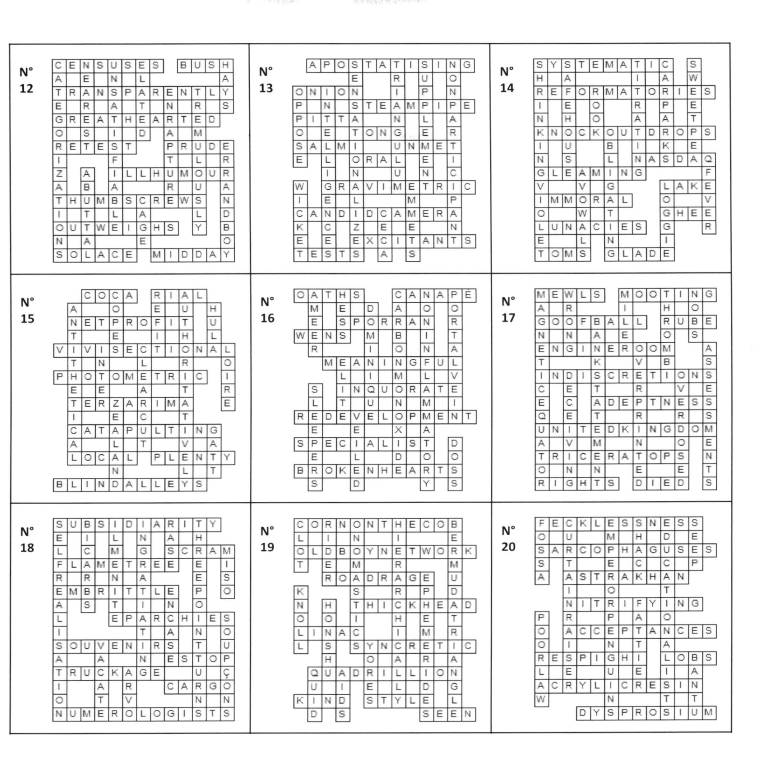

Humble request

dear valued customer
We are a small , family-owned publishing com-
peny and without your support we would not
exist .

Therefor we make a humble request , if you
enjoy this book , please spare a few minutes to
leave us a review on this book's amazon prod-
uct page .

Each and every one of your reviews is para-
mount to our survival and helps us to compete
against larger corporation with bigger market-
ing budget that we do not have .

We are forever gratfull for your support and we
hope we have succeeded in providing your or
your loved one with a very special book .

Made in United States
Troutdale, OR
09/01/2023

12533806R00084